PENGUIN BUSINESS
THE SMART BUSINESS GUIDE TO CHINA E-COMMERCE

Frank Lavin has 30 years of experience helping companies succeed in China, through leadership roles in banking, marketing, and diplomacy. In government, Frank served as US Ambassador to Singapore and US Undersecretary of Commerce for International Trade. In the latter role, he was lead trade negotiator for both China and India and was the senior policy official responsible for commercial policy, export promotion, and trade negotiations.

In the private sector, Frank served as an Asia practice leader at Edelman, and prior to that he worked in senior finance and management positions in Hong Kong and Singapore with Bank of America and Citibank. Frank also served as Chairman of the Steering Committee of the USA Pavilion at the Shanghai 2010 World Expo. Frank is the co-author of "Export Now" (Wiley). Frank earned a B.S. from the School of Foreign Service at Georgetown University; an M.S. in Chinese Language from Georgetown University; an M.A. in International Relations and International Economics from the School of Advanced International Studies at the Johns Hopkins University; and an M.B.A. in Finance at the Wharton School at the University of Pennsylvania.

Frank has a monthly column in Forbes.com, writing about China marketing strategy and current events.

THE SMART BUSINESS GUIDE TO CHINA E-COMMERCE

HOW TO WIN IN THE WORLD'S LARGEST RETAIL MARKET

FRANK LAVIN

BUSINESS

An imprint of Penguin Random House

PENGUIN BUSINESS

USA | Canada | UK | Ireland | Australia
New Zealand | India | South Africa | China | Southeast Asia

Penguin Business is part of the Penguin Random House group of companies
whose addresses can be found at global.penguinrandomhouse.com

Published by Penguin Random House SEA Pte Ltd
9, Changi South Street 3, Level 08-01,
Singapore 486361

First published in Penguin Business by Penguin Random House SEA 2021

Copyright © Frank Lavin 2021

All rights reserved

10 9 8 7 6 5 4 3 2 1

The views and opinions expressed in this book are the author's own and the
facts are as reported by him which have been verified to the extent possible,
and the publishers are not in any way liable for the same.

ISBN 9789814954655

Typeset in Adobe Garamond Pro by Manipal Technologies Limited, Manipal
Printed at Markono Print Media Pte Ltd, Singapore

www.penguin.sg

Contents

Author's Prologue   vii

1. Don't Stand Still   1

Section One
Learning to Walk—for people without a
China background or orientation

2. The Law of Scale   13

3. The Law of Convergence: The Rise of Chinese Consumers   23

4. Your China Strategy: The Most Common Mistake   29

5. Your China Strategy   42

6. From a Product to a Brand   52

Section Two
Starting to Jog—for people who are
thinking about a China strategy

7. How to Court the Chinese Consumer   65

8. Five Decisions Before You Start   77

9. Platforms and Social Media   93

Section Three
How Fast Can You Run?—for people
who are growing nicely in China

10. Holidays And Digital Promotion Strategies   109

11. Risk and Compliance   122

12. The Art of Marketing in China   137

13. Logistics and Finance   152

14. How to Fail in China   160

15. How to Win in China   170

16. From China to the World   178

Acknowledgements   183

Explanation of Terms   185

Author's Prologue

If a man will begin with certainties, he shall end in doubts; but if he will be content to begin with doubts, he shall end in certainties.

—Sir Francis Bacon

Is it okay for your business to go to China? Is it okay to *think* about going to China? And what is going to happen if you go? That's what this whole book is about, so we had better have a frank talk. Businesses around the world seem to show the same vacillating view of China: it is simultaneously the most attractive country as well as the most challenging country to enter into. Why this contradiction?

This dissonance simply reveals the complexity of China. It is indeed the largest retail market in the world, but it can also be the most challenging or even the most uninviting one, as most foreign businesses have no China experience. Beyond this lack of familiarity, there are significant language and cultural gaps, and political differences. After about fifty years of steady, but modest, improvements in US-China relations, the past few years have seen a rather sharp deterioration. With all the trade friction and political differences, how much sense does it make for any business to think seriously about a China strategy?

It's a fair question. Businesses do not want to venture into a new market only to end up in the middle of a quarrel or to find their business opportunities colored by politics.

Foreign views of China have been subject to wide swings of optimism and pessimism across the several centuries of East-West engagement. For much of the nineteenth and twentieth centuries, a positive business view was almost pervasive, with merchants keen to develop commercial ties in this exotic new market. Across that same period, there were times that were almost fatalistically negative, with China beset by turmoil, war, or anti-foreign political movements. Business sentiment shifted from a deterministically positive view to a deterministically negative one. This book rejects both views: that China is fated to be an enemy of the West or that every business day in China will be a sunny day. China remains a land of both considerable opportunity and challenges.

Let me offer a sober assessment: At bad moments, China is never as bad as it might seem and at good moments, China is never as good as it might seem.

If there is a core lesson from this book it is that the emergence of e-commerce allows businesses largely to contain their costs and the risks, whereas the opportunity is open-ended. If the costs are flat and the benefits are growing, at some point, it makes more sense to go to China than to stay away.

Here's where we are today:

1. The political issues are real. The differences are real. Even if the ill-will—or some of it—is accentuated by personalities, the underlying problems are not about to go away quickly.
2. The business environment is good and continues to improve. US sales in China are at record highs. Many global firms are having their best year ever in China, even with the pandemic.* During this entire period of friction, the Chinese government has not taken any steps to harm the sale of foreign consumer goods. No calls for boycotts of US, or any other country's, goods, and no seizures. Business is booming.

---

* In one survey, 33 per cent of US companies projected 2020 to be ahead of 2019, but 49 per cent said it would be worse. https://www.amcham-shanghai.org/en/article/amcham-shanghai-releases-2020-china-business-report

I can sum up these two seemingly contradictory themes with a saying we used when I served as US Undersecretary of Commerce: 'China isn't for wimps.'

In other words, foreign businesses in China are likely to encounter more complications, more unpredictability, and more frustrations than in their home market.

The core point: proceed, but proceed with an all-weather, calibrated strategy that gives your company access to the China market, and limits risks and costs.

What is the desired outcome? The parallel comfort zones

So what is the desired outcome when it comes to starting in China? For me, it has always been about establishing two parallel comfort zones—one for the Chinese consumer and one for the foreign merchant.

The first comfort zone is for the Chinese consumer. This means the product is found on their preferred platform; they can pay with their payment instruments; with account support in their time zone and in their language. The Chinese consumer goes on to enjoy local delivery time and local delivery costs.

So the Chinese consumer can purchase French perfume, Australian wine, German technology, or South Korean cosmetics—and she does not have to navigate a website in France, Australia, Germany, or Korea.

The second comfort zone is for the foreign merchant, be it from the US or elsewhere. The business sells to China, yet it receives payment in its home currency. In the same vein, the merchant's contract is with an offshore entity, and they receive their account support in their language and in their time zone.

In other words, the business can sell into China but they do not need to visit China. They do not need to set up an office or a legal entity in China. They do not need to navigate Chinese labor law or tax law. The business can focus on making the best product, and someone in China can focus on sales, social media, customer contact, and financial settlement.

Neither the Chinese consumer nor the foreign business has to leave their comfort zone.

* * *

By way of background, I have spent most of my career helping companies enter and win in new markets, with a focus on China. I have served in government, banking, and public affairs, and for the past ten years, I have served as Chairman and CEO of Export Now, a US company that runs e-commerce stores in China for international brands, along with market research and other services. At Export Now, we have worked with companies from Fortune 500 to fast-growing start-ups. It has been a joy to introduce Chinese consumers to products that delight consumers around the world. I am glad to draw on my thirty years of China experience to share some insights with you. I am grateful to friends and colleagues from China, the United States, and around the world who also contributed ideas and suggestions for this book, providing data, case studies, and focus-group insight.

The concepts in this book are market-tested and I hope useful, but their application and success will not be the same with every brand. I try to present these insights in the sense of time-honored lessons learned, but there are new lessons every day. Your experience might be different in various respects, but the lessons of the book should still broadly apply.

One final thought: There are always reasons to be pessimistic about China and even about US–China relations, but there are some overwhelming reasons to be positive, and the most important one is the Chinese people. The more time you spend in China, the more respect you will have for their aspirations and their desire for a better life. It is to the Chinese consumer that I dedicate this book. They are transforming their country and the world through their energy and imagination. Let's hope that foreign businesses rise to the occasion and do what they can to learn and participate in this new China.

No, China is not for wimps. You might encounter more heartburn than in other markets. You might have a higher error rate as you encounter the differences between Chinese and American consumers. There is likely to be more volatility in the market as consumer behavior is less 'sticky' as well. And none of this is cost-free. Yet all these problems are more than offset by the extraordinary size and growth of the China market. The destination is worth the journey. It is not just 'okay' to think about China, it is important for every business to do so. Come with me as we take our first steps.

1

Don't Stand Still

The Biggest Party in Shopping

In other countries e-commerce is icing on the cake. In China, it is the cake.

The pace of change is accelerating, and traditional retail is being left behind. The world is not standing still. Technology is not standing still. Your competitors are not standing still. There are new products, new processes, and new markets. The on-demand economy is changing the way we hail rides, order food, and procure services from dog-walking to accounting. Alternative energy companies bring us cheaper and greener energy. Entrepreneurs are launching life-changing businesses from private space travel to cloud computing. And we see similar transformation underway in retail.

Today's retail environment is being shaped by two powerful trends: the rise of e-commerce and the rise of China. This chapter will introduce these two trends and explain how China has transformed consumer behavior and we will give you an insider's look at its tremendous impact by taking you to the biggest shopping day in the world: Singles' Day.

China, the E-Commerce Leader

The idea is pretty simple: E-commerce is the fastest-growing retail channel in the world and China is the fastest-growing market in the world. In fact, China's retail e-commerce grew by 27 per cent in 2019, pushing it to almost 55 per cent of all e-commerce in the world.* Putting these two trends together means that e-commerce significantly reduces the costs and risks for companies to enter and win in China. Given slower growth elsewhere in the world economy, China's e-commerce market might offer the most effective opportunity to grow your company and transform your product into a successful international brand.

Let's look at the role e-commerce plays in China and how it is different from e-commerce in other markets.

In other leading markets, e-commerce is generally seen as a transaction channel, a tool for consumers.

Customers embrace e-commerce because it offers broader choice, better pricing, and greater convenience. In other words, it provides an improved version of what the traditional bricks-and-mortar channel offers. E-commerce flourishes by following consumer demand.

In China, however, e-commerce shapes and leads consumer demand. It serves as an outlet for social media, as a communications channel, and as a platform for games and entertainment.

Tmall is the largest e-commerce platform in China. As Chloe Goncalves, Tmall senior business development manager, explains:

> Consumers in Europe shop online as a way to save time, whereas in China, consumers use Tmall as a way to spend time. On average, consumers open the Tmall and Taobao apps 7 times per day for about 20–30 minutes, with approximately 20 million comments shared daily.†

Consumers in China have access to a wide range of content—from short videos, livestreaming, influencer recommendations, product showcases, even 3D stores—all of which allow them to browse, learn, discover, share, and interact directly with brands. Consumerism is a lifestyle.

This e-commerce ecosystem also helps brands. They now have access to innovative digital tools allowing them to create engaging and tailored shopping experiences. They get real-time statistics and narrative feedback from consumers.

---

* https://www.emarketer.com/content/global-ecommerce-2019
† https://luxuryconversation.com/tmall-niche-luxury-digital-china/

Even if your brand sells through bricks and mortar, your brand is defined, discussed, and evaluated through e-commerce. In other countries e-commerce is icing on the cake. In China, it is the cake.

How did this happen? How did China become the world leader in e-commerce? There are a number of factors behind this impressive growth.

1. Disposable income is on the rise

From 2000 to 2018, China's middle class as among the fastest growing in the world, expanding from 39.1 million people to 707 million.[*]

As China reaches middle income, personal consumption shifts away from necessities and toward discretionary purchases. It is no surprise we see a surge in demand for international lifestyle brands.

Over the years, brands such as Levi's, L'Oréal, Montblanc, and Uniqlo have all met a favorable response in China. The aspirational Chinese consumer has many of the same needs and desires as their overseas counterparts. Uniqlo has 767 stores in China, more than the 764 stores in its home market (Japan). Greater China sales account for 20 per cent of its global revenue.[†] L'Oréal's China sales grew by 35 per cent in 2019, making China its second-largest market.[‡]

2. Physical retailers can lack quality, consistency, and customer service

In the more affluent cities such as Shanghai, Beijing, and Guangzhou, finding a quality shopping mall or grocery store is an easy affair. But for much of China's population, accessing high-quality retail stores can be a challenge. There is growing prosperity in China, but the traditional retail sector is oriented toward the middle-income consumer. Premium goods are harder to find.

---

[*] https://chinapower.csis.org/china-middle-class/

[†] https://asia.nikkei.com/Business/Retail/Uniqlo-has-more-stores-in-China-than-Japan#:~:text=The%20market%20Uniqlo%20calls%20greater,market%20is%20expanding%20rapidly%2C%20however.

[‡] https://daxueconsulting.com/loreal-china/#:~:text=Since%202017%2C%20China's%20cosmetics%20market,36%20billion%20in%20in%202019.

Even when outlets are available, many lack product selection, can run low on inventory, or offer poor customer service. E-commerce gives the broader population access to quality brands that had previously been limited to the larger cities.

3.   China's leading e-commerce sites have a deep grasp of what their consumer base demands

Through peer reviews, creative promotions, and return policies, China's leading e-commerce sites offer an experience that fosters trust and comfort. Websites with a dedicated customer service team and product-availability metrics further contribute to a more enjoyable experience.

Tmall and JD (China's second largest e-commerce platform), allow users to participate in real-time messaging with customer service representatives, and gives them the freedom to return goods within seven days of purchase, no questions asked.

These e-commerce platforms are further strengthened by a powerful network of social media and electronic payment systems. Thanks to this digital ecosystem, the Chinese consumer enjoys near-seamless connectivity between messaging and product discovery, the purchase of the product, and the final payment. WeChat, the biggest social media platform in China, has 1·2 billion monthly active users who send 45 billion messages on this platform every single day.[*] Douyin (known as TikTok in the West), the fast-growing short-video platform, has 580 million daily active users.[†] Almost the same number, about 550 million people in China use Didi (China's Uber) for ride-hailing services.[‡] Of the 805 million Chinese who make online payments, 802 million make them on their phone.[§]

---

[*] https://assets.kawo.com/KAWO-Ultimate-Intro-to-China-Social-Marketing-v1.pdf

[†] https://www.chinainternetwatch.com/30794/douyin-q1-2020/#:~:text=Douyin%2C%20TikTok's%20China%20native%20app,an%20increase%20of%2072.7%25%20YoY.

[‡] https://www.cnbc.com/2019/08/05/chinese-rideshare-giant-didi-makes-big-move-in-driverless-car-race.html#:~:text=Chinese%20ride%2Dhailing%20giant%20Didi,of%20Beijing%20seven%20years%20ago.

[§] https://cnnic.com.cn/IDR/ReportDownloads/202012/P020201201530023411644.pdf, p.2

4. Online marketplaces can have greater integrity than offline outlets

China's leading e-commerce sites guarantee authentic goods and offer a model that ensures brand integrity. Only the brand owner or authorized agent may operate a store on Tmall or JD. This gives brands direct engagement with consumers and complete control over brand position, product slate, and pricing.

Brands like Estée Lauder, Burberry, and Clarins utilize this trust and build an image through Tmall flagship stores. Merchants on JD.com also go through stringent pre-screenings before opening a shop to ensure that customers receive authentic goods.

5. Smartphones are ubiquitous and have become the equipment of choice for Internet shoppers

Most Chinese consumers carry a shopping mall in their pocket: a smartphone. China now boasts over 900 million smartphone users. And over 83 per cent of China ecommerce will be through a smartphone,* compared to 34 per cent in the US.†

Mobile phone users can seamlessly make purchases through apps such as Alipay, Alibaba's online payment platform, or WeChatPay, Tencent's competing digital payment app, knowing that their money will be escrowed until they confirm satisfaction with the delivered goods. These apps are simple and free and give every user immediate e-commerce purchasing power. Additionally, the smarter digital marketing efforts carefully target mobile phone users, designing their campaigns for the small screen, not just for the larger screens of laptops.

---

* https://www.emarketer.com/content/global-historic-first-ecommerce-china-will-account-more-than-50-of-retail-sales

† https://www.emarketer.com/content/smartphones-will-account-for-more-than-one-third-of-e-commerce-sales-in-2019

6. Limited domestic competition, especially in the premium space

As successful as China is, it is just one generation out of poverty and many in China have only recently attained middle-income status, so the domestic market is overwhelmingly oriented to the mass market, price-sensitive consumer. There are not many Chinese consumers purchasing at a shop where their moms or dads shopped.

The more affluent Chinese consumer realizes it is more likely they might have to go overseas for the brand experience he or she desires.

What this book covers

The Smart Business Guide to China E-Commerce is both an introductory book and a how-to book. It provides a general overview of China e-commerce and its considerable success. It also takes the reader through a journey of how to enter and get started in the China market as well as how to move toward long-term success.

The first few chapters are for people without a China background or orientation:

Chapter 2: The Law of Scale. The size of China's e-commerce system and what that means for international business

Chapter 3: The Law of Convergence. How China's economic growth has spurred the demand in China for premium global brands

Chapter 4: The Mistake of Nothing Different. The most common mistake businesses make when they go to China

Chapter 5: The Key Trade-Offs. How to adjust your company and your metrics for China success

The middle group of chapters are for people who are thinking about a China strategy:

Chapter 6: From a Product to a Brand: How companies make the journey from a strong product to a strong brand and why this is particularly important in China

Chapter 7: How to Court the Chinese Consumer. Showing up is not a strategy. You need to actively win the consumer

Chapter 8: Five Questions Before You Start. How to think through initial strategy and trade-offs

Chapter 9: Platforms and Social Media. An overview

And the final part of the book is for people who are growing nicely in China:

Chapter 10: Promotions and Holidays. More important in China than in any other country.

Chapter 11: Risk and Compliance. A factor in every market, but foreign businesses tend to have less familiarity with China

Chapter 12: Marketing and KOLs. We get into the specifics of the China market.

Chapter 13: Logistics and Finance. China has some advantages here over other markets, but you need to adjust.

Chapter 14: How to Fail in China. We can learn more from failure and others' mistakes.

Chapter 15: How to succeed in China: Let's integrate and apply the lessons of this book.

Chapter 16: From China to the World. A China strategy is the key building-block of a global strategy and it will help your home market business as well.

I hope you will find this book useful and stimulating and I hope it leads to a serious discussion about China opportunities in your business. It is not designed to be an encyclopedia of answers, but as Sir Francis Bacon notes in the prologue, it is sometimes better to have all the questions than to have all the answers.

But before we jump into learning about China e-commerce, please come with me to Singles' Day.

Singles' Day—The Main Event

If you'd like to see how the rise of China and the rise of e-commerce combine to produce extraordinary results, then come with me to a party, or to be more accurate, to a national sales celebration: Singles' Day.

Singles' Day—November 11 (11.11 four singles, naturally)—is the largest shopping day in China. Even though it started in China, Singles' Day has already gained appeal in other countries and it is the largest shopping day in the world, Singles' Day sales (GMV) in China ($132 billion)[*] is almost fifteen times greater than Black Friday sales in the US ($9 billion).[†] Brands offer their best bargains. The e-commerce platforms offer their best promotions. And consumers have been saving and searching for bargains, knowing this is their best opportunity.

Singles' Day is not an official government holiday, but a shopping holiday devised to celebrate the fact that more people are living by themselves than ever. So this is the day designated to buy something you need, or might fancy, or are just curious about.

Imagine the crowd appeal, consumerism, and the spectacle of Christmas sales, the Eurovision song contest, and the World Cup, rolled into one big, bright event.

---

[*] https://www.statista.com/statistics/1176984/china-singles-day-sales-gmv/

[†] Note for sales in this book, we typically use the standard e-commerce term of Gross Merchandise Value (GMV), which is the total value of goods sold on the site. https://www.cnbc.com/2020/11/28/black-friday-2020-online-shopping-surges-22percent-to-record-9-billion-adobe-says.html

Singles' Day is a holiday, a consumer extravaganza, a television gala, and a celebration of brand innovation all bundled into one. It takes place on a scale that makes even the most jaded retailer sit up and take notice.

And Singles' Day is capped by a national television gala hosted by Tmall. It's not just the A-list celebrities at the television gala, such as Taylor Swift, David Beckham, leading Korean K-Pop bands, and *Bundesliga* stars, it's also the total sales. On Singles' Day 2020, Alibaba passed $74 billion in sales and JD.com almost hit $41 billion in sales.[*]

Indeed, the $132 billion in Singles' Day[†] is more than what major markets like the UK ($99 billion) and Japan ($79 billion) sell online in an entire year.[‡]

It's not hard to participate in Singles' Day if you are an international brand. But you cannot merely show up. We'll talk more about Singles' Day in Chapter 10, but the key point is: You need a plan. Indeed, the fastest-growing brands in the world have an international e-commerce strategy and a China strategy—so should you. Don't stand still.

Key Takeaways

➢ Even if your brand sells through bricks and mortar, your brand is defined, discussed, and evaluated through e-commerce.

➢ *Consumers around the world shop online as a way to save time, whereas in China, consumers use Tmall as a way to spend time.* E-commerce is so dominant that it transforms consumer and merchant behavior.

➢ China is perhaps the most digital nation in the world, with smartphones and apps used in every walk of life.

---

[*] https://www.cnbc.com/2020/11/12/singles-day-2020-alibaba-and-jd-rack-up-record-115-billion-of-sales.html.

[†] https://www.statista.com/statistics/1176984/china-singles-day-sales-gmv/

[‡] https://www.business.com/articles/10-of-the-largest-ecommerce-markets-in-the-world-b/

Section One

Learning to Walk—for people without a China background or orientation

2

The Law of Scale

With the Chinese, the business is really moving from strength to strength.
—LVMH Financial Director Jean-Jacques Guiony[*]

Some of these numbers from China are staggering:

- There are fifty million people in the world who are taking piano lessons, and forty million of them are in China.[†]
- US auto manufacturer General Motors sells more cars in China than in the US.[‡]
- There are over 52,000 km of high-speed rail in the world, from France's TGV to Japan's Bullet Train, but 68 per cent of the world's high-speed rail is in China.[§]
- The short video platform Douyin (TikTok) has acquired over 600 million daily active users since its 2016 launch.[¶]

---

[*] https://www.reuters.com/article/us-lvmh-results/lvmh-shares-hit-record-high-as-china-demand-boosts-luxury-group-idUSKCN1RN0LD

[†] http://www.xinhuanet.com/english/2019-03/19/c_137906715.htm

[‡] https://www.statista.com/statistics/304367/vehicle-sales-of-general-motors-by-country/

[§] https://www.globalrailwayreview.com/article/112553/perpetual-growth-high-speed-rail/#:~:text=Today%2C%20the%20high%2Dspeed%20network,world's%20high%2Dspeed%20rail%20network

[¶] https://www.cnbc.com/2020/09/15/bytedance-douyin-has-600-million-daily-active-users.html

- China accounts for 56 per cent of the global sales of 5G smartphones.[*]

As you go through these statistics, you begin to get a sense of the enormous economic transformation of China, of a nation that is growing, building, aspirational, and hungry for a better life. Most important, it is large: with a large population, a large land mass, and a large economy.

Indeed, the most important law that governs business success in China is the *Law of Scale*, meaning the numbers in China are so large that even if your brand has only a fraction of its home market share, it can still be a success.

The commercial truth—and one that we have established since the very beginning of the book—is that, although China is the second-largest economy in the world (behind the US), it is the largest e-commerce market in the world.

By 2020, China's 940 million Internet users (two-thirds of the population) were spending an average of four hours a day online.[†] The US, has a higher Internet penetration—87 per cent, but with a smaller population than China, this translates into 288 million Internet users[‡] out of 331 million people.[§] More significant than e-commerce sales is the e-commerce growth rate. The 11.5 per cent growth rate of China's online retail sales[¶] is more than double the 5 per cent of China' total retail sales growth.[**]

And there is more evidence for the *Law of Scale*.

[*] https://www.statista.com/statistics/1215263/5g-smartphone-market-share-by-country/

[†] https://cnnic.com.cn/IDR/ReportDownloads/202012/P020201201530023411644.pdf

[‡] https://datareportal.com/reports/digital-2020-united-states-of-america#:~:text=There%20were%20288.1%20million%20internet,at%2087%25%20in%20January%202020.

[§] https://www.pbs.org/newshour/nation/3-ways-that-the-u-s-population-will-change-over-the-next-decade#:~:text=The%20U.S.%20population%20today%2C%20at,just%20under%201.4%20billion%2C%20respectively.

[¶] https://www.chinainternetwatch.com/30910/retail-sales/

[**] https://tradingeconomics.com/china/retail-sales-annual

Size of the Economy

Top Ten Countries by GDP[*]	—	trillions of US dollars
(World Bank, 2019)		
1. United States	—	21·3
2. China	—	14·3
3. Japan	—	5·0
4. Germany	—	3·8
5. India	—	2·8
6. United Kingdom	—	2·8
7. France	—	2·7
8. Italy	—	2·0
9. Brazil	—	1·8
10. Canada	—	1·7

Chinese Imports

As a reflection of Chinese consumer demand from around the world, China's imports doubled from $1 trillion to $2 trillion between 2009–2019.[†] Look at some examples:

- Australian winemaker Treasury Wine Estates, spearheaded by the Penfolds label, has China as its biggest market, taking up 30 per cent of its total sales in 2019. [‡]
- One third of P&G's sales growth was from China in 2019.[§]
- 10 per cent of sales of Japanese electronics manufacturer Panasonic comes from China, the same share of its sales to the whole of Europe.[¶]

---

[*] https://data.worldbank.org/indicator/NY.GDP.MKTP.CD

[†] https://www.statista.com/statistics/263646/import-of-goods-to-china/

[‡] https://www.bloomberg.com/news/articles/2020-11-29/treasury-wine-to-divert-labels-from-china-as-169-tariffs-bite

[§] https://www.caixinglobal.com/2019-11-07/one-third-of-pgs-sales-growth-comes-from-china-local-head-says-101480198.html

[¶] https://news.panasonic.com/global/press/data/2020/05/en200518-2/en200518-2-1.pdf

Retail E-Commerce Sales

Finally, China is the world's largest e-commerce market, with triple the sales of the US.[*]

Top 10 Countries, Ranked by Retail E-commerce Sales[†]

	2018	2019	per cent Change
1. China	1·52 Trillion	$1·93 Trillion	27.3
2. United States	515 Billion	587 Billion	14.0
3. United Kingdom	128 Billion	142 Billion	10.9
4. Japan	111 Billion	115 Billion	4.0
5. South Korea	88 Billion	103 Billion	18.1
6. Germany	76 Billion	82 Billion	7.8
7. France	62 Billion	69 Billion	11.5
8. Canada	41 Billion	50 Billion	21.1
9. India	35 Billion	46 Billion	31.9
10. Russia	23 Billion	27 Billion	18.7

Digital Nation

In China, the battle with traditional media is over and the Internet has won. Not only is the scale large in China when one looks at the economy, the size of the retail market, or e-commerce, but China's scale is also large when compared to old media and traditional communications channels.

Chinese ad spending has shifted away from traditional media and into digital marketing for a straightforward reason: that is where the customers are. Chinese consumers spend a large amount of their leisure time online— up to 70 per cent.[‡] This leads to newspaper advertising revenue dropping from RMB 42·5 billion to under RMB 7 billion between 2013 and 2019, while online advertising revenue hit RMB 646 billion in 2019.[§]

---

[*] https://sg.oberlo.com/statistics/ecommerce-sales-by-country

[†] https://www.emarketer.com/content/global-ecommerce-2019

[‡] https://www.mckinsey.com/business-functions/marketing-and-sales/our-insights/chinas-internet-obsession

[§] https://www.statista.com/topics/5604/advertising-in-china/

Smartphone Nation

And within the Internet, the competition between smartphones, laptops, and desktops is over, and smartphones have won. Consumers are using smartphones to voraciously consume social media, news, videos and especially to shop. This means there are 747 million mobile shoppers in China and 309 million of them participate in livestream e-commerce.[*]

How Chinese Netizens Access the Internet[†]

Mobile phones, 99.2 per cent
Desktop computers, 37.3 per cent
Laptop computers, 31.8 per cent
Televisions, 28.6 per cent
Tablet computers, 27.5 per cent

China's smartphone adaptation was driven by a confluence of three developments. The first two were the decrease in smartphone costs during the 2010s as incomes rose. This spurred a more rapid and wider 4G and 5G adoption than the West, which in turn (the third of the three developments) allowed for high-quality video and music content to be streamed and high-quality games to be played. Over one third of mobile phone sales in China are 5G[‡] while in the United States 5G is only about 20 per cent of phone sales.[§] So, in China, phones evolved from communication devices into high-tech entertainment devices. In the United States, when we want to be entertained at the end of the day, we turn on Netflix; Chinese consumers open up the Taobao app.

How many users are using their mobile phones to browse the Internet? Try over 99 per cent.[¶]

---

[*] https://cnnic.com.cn/IDR/ReportDownloads/202012/P020201201530023411644.pdf

[†] https://cnnic.com.cn/IDR/ReportDownloads/202012/P020201201530023411644.pdf, p. 1.

[‡] https://www.zdnet.com/article/5g-smartphone-sales-in-china-are-absolutely-rocketing/

[§] https://www.prnewswire.com/news-releases/5g-smartphones-account-for-14-of-total-us-smartphone-sales-in-aug-301147659.html

[¶] https://cnnic.com.cn/IDR/ReportDownloads/202012/P020201201530023411644.pdf

I mentioned earlier that the average Chinese netizen spends four hours daily online, but how does that break down by activity?

How Chinese Netizens Spend Their Time Online[*]

Instant messaging, 13.7 per cent
Video, 12.8 per cent
Audio, 10.9 per cent
Video clips, 8.8 per cent
Music, 8.1 per cent
Livestreaming apps, 7.3 per cent

Ecosystem Nation

China's major online hubs interconnect with news portals, games, videos, and e-commerce, offering 'click-to-buy' product placements that are simple and fast for consumers.

Alibaba, for example, is no longer simply running online marketplaces where merchants just place search ads. Its investments in other outlets like video site Youku—China's YouTube counterpart—means Alibaba's e-commerce platforms are now 'lifestyle channels' that are part of a larger media ecosystem.

Within this ecosystem, consumers can find a wide range of information and entertainment, interact with celebrities, opinion leaders, brands and each other; and participate in online communities. If you are looking for a date, you can go on the Tantan dating app, which has 360 million users and has created 15 billion matches since it was launched in 2014.[†] If you are looking for lifestyle information such as makeup, fashion, and smarter living tips, there is a platform just for you: Xiaohongshu. Its success has allowed it to capture some 300 million users, or 90 per cent of female netizens.[‡]

---

[*] https://cnnic.com.cn/IDR/ReportDownloads/202012/P020201201530023411644.pdf

[†] https://kr-asia.com/chinese-dating-app-tantan-claims-360-million-registered-users-but-no-profits

[‡] https://daxueconsulting.com/latest-facts-and-insights-about-xiaohongshu/#:~:text=QuestMobile's%20data%20shows%2C%20the%20number,%2D%20and%202nd%2D%20tier%20cities.

This environment not only offers marketers more options for reaching and engaging customers where they live online through multiple multimedia channels; the ecosystem's 'one-stop-shop' nature also can simplify the development of digital marketing campaigns. This translates into more time online.

Alibaba CEO Daniel Zhang says that the average mobile Taobao user spends more than twenty minutes a day on the app, compared with Amazon mobile users' average of 8.9 minutes, according to media research firm ComScore.[*]

China's big online marketplaces are leading the world in the use of data and analytics to target and understand customers. Unlike Western marketplaces like Amazon, Alibaba allows merchants to 'own' their relationship with their customers, giving them access to specific data through value-added services that lets merchants to do their own analysis using Alibaba software and tools.

With nearly 933 million mobile Internet users, the type of information Alibaba collects includes data on shopping habits, payment and credit history, search preferences, social networks, and interests—drawing on information gleaned from individual activity throughout the Alibaba ecosystem. This ability to understand and zoom in on specific customer wants and needs can greatly increase marketing effectiveness and foster stronger customer relationships.

However, One Caveat

The one caveat is that, while China's e-commerce sales are about three times as much as that of the US, China has a lower per capita GDP. Of China's 940 million Internet users, about 75 per cent of them have a monthly income of under RMB 5000 (almost $735).[†] Since China's purchasing power is lower, this means you will have to adapt your marketing and targeting strategies.

---

[*] https://www.chyxx.com/industry/202009/896630.html
[†] https://cnnic.com.cn/IDR/ReportDownloads/202012/P020201201530023411644.pdf

This is where the *Law of Scale* makes a difference in your favor. If 75 per cent of consumers in the US have the purchasing power to afford your products, but only 12 per cent of consumers do in China, that is over 100 million Internet shoppers. Not a bad target market, but you need to remember that in the US your 75 per cent target would make you a mass market brand, whereas in China your 12 per cent target makes you more of a premium or niche brand.

And that 12 per cent is growing nicely. In other words, purchasing power in China is among the fastest growing in the world. So, if you are targeting only 12 per cent of the population this year, you will be targeting 13–14 per cent next year. No surprise that foreign consumer goods sales were growing by 9.5 per cent in 2019 compared to a Chinese company growth of 7 per cent.[*]

There is even more of a skew in the luxury segment of the market. A Bain study tells us that,

> As a region, mainland China will account for 28 percent of the luxury market, up from 11 percent in 2019.[†]

And the future looks even brighter as Chinese consumers should account for nearly half of all purchases worldwide by 2025.[‡§] The boom in luxury is likely spurred by inter-related drivers of income growth, increased consumer awareness of international brands, and ongoing marketing efforts of those brands—topics we will explore throughout this book.

Large and Getting Larger

It's not just that the numbers in China are large. They are likely to continue to outpace world norms for the near future. Given that 500 million of China's 1·4 billion are not on the Internet, there's still room for growth. Once you take out those off-line shoppers and also subtract

---

[*] https://www.bain.com/insights/in-2019-foreign-brands-outgrew-chinese-brands-in-china-snap-chart/

[†] https://www.bain.com › about › spring-luxury-report

[‡] https://www.bain.com/about/media-center/press-releases/2020/spring-luxury-report/

[§] https://www.bain.com/about/media-center/press-releases/2020/spring-luxury-report/

the emergency purchases of lightbulbs and cigarettes, this means a solid majority of premium and mass-premium goods in China are sold online.

We see the same phenomenon in both the US and China. People are creatures of habit and if you did not grow up with e-commerce, you might not prefer it—until your habitual retail channel is disrupted.

People like e-commerce for the same reason they like email, social media, and online banking. It's a better deal with better selection, better data, comparisons and reviews, better experimentation, better customer experience, and better social connectivity. You have more choices on Amazon alone to buy your jeans—brands, colors, sizes, and prices—than you do offline.

And for businesses, e-commerce is a better solution as well—less expensive to operate, faster, better margins, easier experimentation and product introduction. Plus it provides all sorts of opportunities for educating consumers and building a brand identity.

In the post-Covid-19 world, the shopping equation has changed. Yes, the world has been turned upside down. Many US and European brands are a bit shell-shocked by the disruption in their home markets. They never needed to think about international expansion. Now with the home market battered, it is time to start.

A kitchen accessory company in Pennsylvania told me that 60 per cent of their sales were through Bed, Bath, and Beyond. Terrific news—until BB&B closed its doors. Sure, they will reopen, but it is quite a disruption for the accessory company.

Meanwhile, 8,000 miles away, several hundred million kitchens are just waiting for new brands. No surprise this company is moving smartly into e-commerce and starting to think about overseas markets.

As Daniel Zhang said in September 2020 during Alibaba Investor Day:

> In the midst of so many uncertainties, the future of digitalization is the biggest certainty we can see. Digitalization is the biggest opportunity of our time.[*]

---

[*] https://www.alizila.com/alibaba-investor-day-2020-daniel-zhang-sees-digitalization-as-the-biggest-opportunity-of-our-time/

The escalating trade tensions between the US and China is one of those uncertainties. But China will undoubtedly continue to be an attractive market because of its size. China is around 55 per cent of global e-commerce and the United States is at about 17 per cent,* so a strategy that is just US–China centered still gets you around 72 per cent of global e-commerce and about 40 per cent of global GDP.

E-commerce, of course, allows international brands to enter the market without ever opening up physical distribution. It's still possible to sell into China without any personnel or facilities there.

Premium and specialty brands are likely to continue enjoying strong sales in China because the country is developing a sophisticated consumer culture. And Chinese consumers have a strong appetite for premium brands. From Zara to Starbucks to Estée Lauder, American and international brands should excel in the mass-premium and premium space. The numbers are in their favor.

Key Takeaways

> The numbers in China are huge. *The Law of Scale* tells us there is no other market in the world that offers the e-commerce opportunity that China offers.

> This good news is somewhat offset because you are speaking to a smaller segment of the market to reflect the lower per capita purchasing power in China.

> E-commerce is the bridge between these two points. It allows the merchant to decide with whom it will engage. The reach, sales, and engagement of e-commerce is on a long-term positive growth trajectory as society becomes more digital.

> China leads the world in this evolution. China's economy will continue to out-perform the global average over the near-term, making China one of the stronger components of global growth for international companies.

---

* https://sg.oberlo.com/statistics/ecommerce-sales-by-country

3

The Law of Convergence: The Rise of Chinese Consumers

How to Measure Brand Strength

There is one cup of Starbucks in the world.

The first law governing e-commerce success is the *Law of Scale* and the second law is the *Law of Convergence*. The *Law of Convergence* holds that consumer tastes around the world tend to converge, assuming purchasing power parity.

The success of great global brands—from Mercedes-Benz to Starbucks, from Crest to Johnnie Walker—is only possible because consumers have somewhat similar preferences, which is why we say tastes tend to converge: 65 per cent of Illy Coffee sales takes place outside of Italy;[*] 86 per cent of Mercedes Benz sales takes place outside of Germany;[†] 83 per cent of Toyota's 2020 sales are outside of Japan.[‡]

The good news for brands is that consumers in China tend to behave in similar fashion with other consumers around the world at the same income level. In other words, your brand tends to convey the same value

---

[*] https://www.ft.com/content/41d38642-6b49-11e9-80c7-60ee53e6681d

[†] https://www.best-selling-cars.com/brands/2019-full-year-global-mercedes-benz-sales-worldwide/

[‡] https://www.automotiveworld.com/news-releases/toyotas-global-sales-and-production-up-year-on-year-in-october-for-second-consecutive-month/

proposition with a similar consumer group in China as it does in your home market.

Brand Integrity

The great global brands understand the Law of Convergence and maintain brand integrity when they enter China. They offer the same value proposition and the same product.

One key to Starbucks' international success is that there is one cup of coffee in the world. Starbucks strives for an identical coffee at all Starbucks locations, whether in Seattle, Paris, or Shanghai. There is no 'China Starbucks' but there is Starbucks in China. There is no 'emerging market Starbucks' but there is Starbucks in the emerging markets. Brand integrity is key, and it starts with consistency across markets.

Mercedes-Benz started producing cars in China through a joint venture in 2005, and they have followed the same principle. They don't craft an inferior version of their automobiles for the China market. They brought their best-selling models, vehicles that stand for quality and luxury. It's for this reason, that despite a global pandemic, Daimler saw a 24 per cent increase in Chinese demand for its Mercedes-Benz cars.[*]

Your Prospects

Chinese consumers want your product for the same reason that consumers in your home market do. You do not have to change—indeed, you should not change—your brand identity. However, the value of brand integrity still does not answer the most important question for any brand thinking about China: How successful will my brand be in the China market?

This is not a question particular to China, but China tends to cause international brands the greatest concern due to lack of familiarity. A brand that has been selling in France and Germany should be able to model its success in other European markets reasonably well and should

---

[*] https://www.reuters.com/article/daimler-results/update-5-daimler-lifts-profit-forecast-as-china-snaps-up-luxury-cars-idUSL8N2HE0VK

even be able to shed some light on North America and other developed markets. But when it comes to China, many companies are in unknown territory.

There are five criteria for evaluating a brand's prospects in China:

1. **Brand strength**: Is your product a differentiated product or are you largely competing on price? Price competition is a dead end in China because the local brands will likely offer low-cost products. It'll be a race to the bottom, and you'll likely lose. Here's one test of a brand's strength: If a person receives your product as a gift, would they tell a friend? Most successful apparel brands, for example, pass this test. Consumers are proud to have the newest fashion and will readily share that information.

2. **Digital Reach**: As mentioned in Chapter 2, China is a digital nation, more so than the United States or European nations. Chinese consumers evaluate products, check reviews, and purchase online more than consumers from any other country. You need a digital strategy including social media and, perhaps even a strategy that allows you to sell seamlessly between digital channels and traditional stores, called 'omnichannel'. All successful brands have a story, but they are not all equally successful in communicating it. In China, you need to tell your story and you need to do it digitally. Is digital in your DNA, or have you grown your company through the traditional distributor and retail channels? Brands that have strong consumer e-commerce sales in their home markets tend to fare well in China, so make sure that you have your digital house in order domestically before entering this highly competitive market.

3. **International Footing**: Does your company have international competency? If your brand is already sold in multiple countries, you have the base-line capabilities. Your shipping department can deal with customs declarations. Your finance department understands foreign exchange and remittance. Your marketing team knows you have to localize your brand. But if you have never entered a new market, you need to make sure that you are properly allocating the extra resources necessary. In other words, do not simply treat China as a large version of Ohio or a province in your home market. As you start to build

your brand in China, realize that you will have to disproportionately emphasize your communications and other brand-building activities. Even if you are a market leader domestically, you are a start-up in China.

4. **Customer Loyalty**: Do you have a relationship with your customers? Would your customers post a picture of your product on social media? Do you communicate with them and respond to their communications? Retail experts and statisticians have developed the concept of a 'Net Promoter Score®' an indicator which measures the likelihood of a consumer recommending the product.* One of the more powerful changes in consumer advertising over the past few decades is that brands are less likely to talk 'to' the consumer and more likely to talk 'with' the consumer, fostering a more intimate relationship. Successful brands are in a permanent conversation with their customers. Food product companies sponsor cooking competitions. Luxury brands host wine tastings. And social media makes this an everyday occurrence.

5. **Management Commitment**: How robust is your management? Are they dedicated to success in a new market, particularly if that market requires a long-term approach? In my experience, companies need to attain a certain size and maturity before they can focus on new market entry. They also need to have the endurance and appetite for the competition and complexity. Small companies can certainly enter foreign markets, but it requires dedication and focus and that can be a reach.

Not every brand succeeds in China on the e-commerce route but, as the prosperity of the market continues to grow, as the cost of market entry continues to drop, and as tastes grow and converge, sooner or later China is likely to end up on your 'to do' list.

---

* Reichheld, Fred, Markey, Rob. *The Ultimate Question 2.0: How Net Promoter Companies Thrive in a Customer-Driven World*, Boston, Mass.: Harvard Business Review Press, 2011, p. 52.

National Football League

Some brands and activities are more dependent on a particular culture, and thus have a longer journey in order to be adopted in a new market. But the story of the National Football League in China illustrates that the that journey is possible. The NFL came to my company Export Now with a simple request: Can you help sell footballs in China? The problem was that the NFL was promoting community teams, municipal leagues, and club teams at schools, but the players could not readily acquire the footballs they needed. The NFL did not have a business licence to engage in trading activity, so they came to Export Now and we set up the NFL's first stores in China and helped them in the early days of building out their base.

If you only looked at the warm reception in China to America's National Basketball Association or the English Premier League you might think that Chinese people like watching international sports, but this is only partially correct. The NFL is not the NBA or the EPL.

There are a series of reasons why the NFL has a smaller fan base in China. As a contact sport, it is less appealing to many Chinese parents. Because it requires more equipment, it is harder to start a team, whereas even the most remote village in China will have a field where kids can kick a ball around. Its US game schedules don't make it easy for the Chinese to watch the games. There are not many Chinese players playing in the NFL. Even Tom Brady— arguably the greatest football quarterback of all time—is surpassed in popularity in China by his wife Gisele Bündchen. Well, China is a fashion-forward country.

Nonetheless, the NFL is growing steadily in popularity, in part because the arrival of streamed entertainment means people can watch the games they choose regardless of the time zone.

I got a little more insight into this strategy when I was presenting in Hong Kong and one of the other presenters happened to be former NFL Commissioner Paul Tagliabue. I introduced myself and talked about what we were doing with the NFL in China. My guess was that much of the China initiative was spurred by what he had done with the NFL in Europe, setting up a local league, getting the games on television, and arranging exhibition games.

Paul agreed that the NFL learned a lot from the Europe experience and then he told me how the story began. He had been on a basketball scholarship at Georgetown University when basketball was played at the 1960 Rome Olympics. In 1960, Italy was one of the sixteen countries competing in the basketball finals to the surprise and delight of the host population, most of whom were unfamiliar with the game. Immediately after the Olympics, Italy formed a national basketball association, and it became a popular sport. This showed Paul that sports popularity could be transferred across cultures. When he arrived at the NFL, he had to decide whether football would be a one-country sport or a global sport. He started the journey to Europe and set the stage for a China expansion.

Key Takeaways

➤ If there is magic in the brand, the magic can work in China. If your product works in your home market, the odds are it will also work in China, although perhaps not to the same extent.

➤ You will appeal to the same demographic segment as in your home market, which for premium and luxury goods will be a smaller percentage of the population, but could be larger in absolute terms. Don't go down-market in the hopes of chasing customers. Don't dilute quality or customer service. Don't weaken the value proposition.

4

Your China Strategy: The Most Common Mistake

Copy decisions made by Chicago-based bosses without passports do not go down smoothly in China.[*]

—Tom Doctoroff

The Law of Convergence discusses what is likely to work in China. In this chapter we will discuss what is likely not to work in China. Most successful brands share two common experiences, but this success might have taught them the wrong lessons.

The first experience that teaches the wrong lesson is that their growth has been overwhelmingly organic. Every year, the brand has been making more, selling more, hiring more, advertising more, and earning more. This is a nice success story that has been largely constant across the history of the company. This company's mantra is MOTS—*More of the Same*, a reasonable starting point.

The second experience that teaches the wrong lesson is that the growth has been overwhelmingly in the home market. A fair number of companies in the US and Europe start as family businesses and over the years become increasingly professional and effective in core operations, with lessons learned in production, marketing, distribution, and finance. But there have

---

[*] Doctoroff, Tom, *Billions*, St Martin's Publishing Group, Kindle Edition, 2015, p. 199.

been no lessons learned in market entry or international strategy because the company has never undertaken market entry or international strategy. Even when there is international activity, it tends to be in homogenous societies. A German firm will first expand to Switzerland and Austria, or a US firm will expand to Canada.

If you put these two experiences together, it is easy to conclude that expansion is a natural process, and that business practices and consumer behavior are identical in every market.

This is the most common mistake in international expansion—*the Mistake of Nothing Different*—that international expansion is just a version of domestic expansion, and that it is driven by a MOTS view of business.

The approach of 'nothing different' is generally accurate in terms of domestic development. If your company grew from London to Manchester to Birmingham over the last few years, you probably did not have to make a lot of adjustments in your model. There might well have been nothing you had to adjust, nothing to change, nothing to modify or adapt.

But in entering a foreign market, the mistake of nothing different is a perilous route. In other words, the worst decision—the biggest blunder—a brand can make is treating another country as if it were identical to its home market and not making any changes in its business practices.

Brands enter China without changing anything, not their product selection, their competitive analysis, their advertising spend, or their time horizon. For an example of how to adapt and localize for the China market, look at what Estée Lauder did.

Estée Lauder case study

Estée Lauder is one of the great beauty brands. A global success story, it knew it had to adjust and localize for the China market. It took a three-step approach:

1. New Brand. Estée Lauder launched a skincare brand called Osiao in Hong Kong in 2012. This brand was specially designed for North Asian skin.*

2. Digital Marketing. Estée Lauder's CEO Fabrizio Freda states that 75 per cent of investments were spent on digital marketing and social media. Estée Lauder had an extensive messaging effort on RED (Xiaohongshu) during Singles' Day 2020.†

3. Key Opinion Leaders (KOLs). Yang Mi, a famous Chinese actress, is Estée Lauder's brand ambassador. Her 2020 livestream for Singles' Day had more than 3·6 million views.‡ Meanwhile, the cosmetics brand also engaged in KOL marketing in China. In the 2019 Singles' Day presales, Chinese actress Li Jiaqi sold 4,00,000 units of Estée Lauder's Advanced Night Repair in a few minutes of livestream.§

Brand Innovation, digital marketing, and celebrities means: youth. By aiming specifically for Chinese consumers, by communicating digitally, and by using youthful KOLs, Estée Lauder has repositioned its brand for the youth segment.

China's Not Ohio, Nor Canada, Nor France: Lessons from Adaptation

If the Mistake of Nothing Different is the most frequent mistake companies make when trying to reach new customers abroad, why is it so common? I think it is the appeal of the familiar.

---

* https://www.elcompanies.com/en/news-and-media/newsroom/press-releases/2012/10-3-2012#:~:text=NEW%20YORK%20%2D%2D(BUSINESS%20WIRE,skin's%20youthful%20luster%20and%20light.

† https://www.thedrum.com/news/2019/08/20/est-e-lauder-now-spends-huge-portion-its-marketing-budget-influencers

‡ https://www.alizila.com/how-brands-can-turn-11-11-innovation-into-yearlong-success/

§ https://www.shangyexinzhi.com/article/299524.html

Faced with the uncertainties of selling to unfamiliar consumers, company executives often decide that the best way to avoid missteps is to just keep doing what has worked for them in the past. In other words, they change nothing. They don't adjust product offerings, pricing, distribution, marketing strategy—everything stays in the comfort zone. Simply put, the company treats a promising new market like China as if it were a much larger version of Ohio.

Lessons from Canada

This Mistake of Nothing Different usually comes about because companies have enjoyed success at home by standardizing many aspects of their businesses. Yet this approach can be precisely the wrong one when going abroad. Big-box retailer Target made the mistake when it set its sights on the Canadian market. Target was so committed to its US inventory playbook that it did not allow its Canadian employees to restock shelves with substitute products when the company's regular inventory was not available. As a result, Canadian shoppers encountered empty shelves.

Given the close similarities between Canada and the US, Target's initial approach had a certain logic. Unlike their neighbors to the south, however, Canadian shoppers tend to go to separate stores for grocery, pharmaceutical, and general needs. To persuade them to adopt the one-stop-shopping habit, Target needed to provide a phenomenal customer experience. Instead, when people went to Target Canada, they could not consistently find the products they wanted, making a poor first impression. Because no adjustments were made for local product preferences and shopping style, Target Canada never got any traction with consumers. Target ended up by closing all of its 133 Canadian stores.

Lessons from France

Another example: Starbucks in France. French café culture emphasizes sitting down and enjoying time spent sipping a drink, preferably espresso. A customer would visit their nearby café and be served their 'usual' order by a waiter they had known for years. In contrast, Starbucks offers a grab-and-go style, featuring Americanos in disposable cups.

So, Starbucks made changes. They had employees wear name tags and take customer's names with orders to improve personal familiarity (a practice which spread to other countries as well). Stores also provided more seating and introduced a lighter 'blonde' espresso roast to account for complaints that Starbucks's espresso tasted too charred. Starbucks also upgraded the interior decor at their outlets to make them look less like a fast-food outlet. The result? Starbucks turned a money-losing operation into a profitable one.

Lessons from China: E-commerce as a research tool

We should understand that every market is unique and deserves customized treatment. In countries such as China, foreign firms must be particularly mindful of differences in culture, purchasing power, and consumer preferences. Yet many companies don't try to adapt because they lack the analytical tools to understand the differences between their home market and the China market—tools that are in fact readily accessible to retailers selling through e-commerce.

By entering a new market online, companies can get sales data in real time. They can adjust for consumer preferences and make changes to account for trends far more quickly. Additionally, online merchants require less inventory and have lower logistical and set-up costs. Finally, companies can easily test communication themes and promotional strategies online. Once a company has a strong e-commerce presence, it can expand to offline channels with a dataset of knowledge as to what works. E-commerce is simply the fastest and least-expensive testbed for experimentation and learning.

Look at China again, where consumer behavior is overwhelmingly a social experience. Consumers share results and purchases on social media. They participate in buying clubs and group purchases. They are rewarded for social feedback. Consumers search for reviews and comments before purchases. This provides every e-commerce merchant with a running commentary on their products and operations.

For example, my company, Export Now, worked with the National Football League (NFL) in their China social media strategy. With more than 4,00,000 followers on Sina Weibo, the Chinese version of Twitter, the NFL receives an excellent flow of information about which teams and players are trending. In turn, this allows us to more effectively manage inventory and anticipate demand. The top requirement for companies in new markets is hard data on consumers. E-commerce gets you there.

If you want to win in China or any new market, e-commerce will help you make the adjustment from your home market as rapidly and as inexpensively as possible. E-commerce is not just a sales tool, it is also a planning and a strategy tool. It allows you to feel the pulse of the new market and to avoid the Mistake of Nothing Different.

Wait a Sec—What about Starbucks and the Law of Convergence?

The Mistake of Nothing Different—that you should not enter China without making changes—seems to contradict the Law of Convergence— that strong brands offer the same value proposition in China as in their home market. What gives?

Both points are true even though they might seem to be somewhat contradictory.

The French Roast you purchase in Starbucks Shanghai is indeed the same French Roast you will get in any other Starbucks in the world. Same roasting and brewing procedure. Same beans. Same service. Same great coffee.

But Starbucks made several adaptations to their positioning when they entered China:

—They originated a series of snacks and pastries based on Chinese preferences, such as green tea cake.

—They built promotions around Chinese holidays.

—They devised a mobile app and home delivery, allowing it to compete directly with an aggressive local start-up, Luckin.

—They enabled digital payments through QR codes.

In other words, Starbucks adapted a successful model to the market conditions it found, modifying its strategy, its communications, its products, and its distribution.

Starbucks realized it needed to offer home delivery for four reasons. First, the local competitor was offering it. Second, delivery costs were sufficiently low (under $1) that it would not impede overall sales. Third, because coffee is a less popular drink in China than in the US, fewer homes and businesses have a coffee machine or coffee service. Finally, there is a stronger food delivery culture in China than in western markets, so it is more of an accepted commercial norm.

Starbucks executed a shrewd understanding that the Law of Convergence and the Mistake of Nothing Different are not contradictory but inherently intertwined.

E-commerce and the Single-brand Store

One of the more interesting examples of how e-commerce has changed consumer behavior, and thereby brand behavior, is the impact it has had on multi-brand stores. In the last few years, leading retailers such as Best Buy, the Home Depot, and Neiman-Marcus have all closed their China stores. Yet, during this same period, foreign brands such as Nike, Levi's, and Starbucks have seen strong increases in China sales. How can these two developments take place at the same time?

The explanation in part lies in the impact that online shopping is having on department stores and multi-brand retailers. This impact has been particularly pronounced in China, where sales at general merchandise stores, while rising in absolute terms, has been falling as a share of all retailing, according to a report from Fung Business Intelligence Centre:

> This sector is losing share of retail spend as it confronts heightened competition, including from fast-growing Internet pure plays.*

That's another way of saying that the advantage of one-stop-shopping, something that in the bricks-and-mortar era was a

---

* https://www.fbicgroup.com/sites/default/files/Global%20Department%20Store%20Report%20by%20FBIC%20Global%20Retail%20Tech%2006_13_2015.pdf

strength of multi-brand retailers, is being undermined by the variety of products offered by China's vibrant e-commerce marketplaces and the convenience of online comparison shopping.

For example, in the US if you want to buy a GoPro camera, a consumer would typically visit a camera, sporting goods, or Best Buy website. In China, consumers are more likely to go directly to the source and shop on the GoPro flagship e-commerce store, where they can pose questions to a live customer service rep, read product reviews, and compare and purchase almost any GoPro model.

It's the same story for cosmetics, housewares, and snack products. Chinese consumers tend to visit the L'Oréal, Kohler, or Wrigley flagship e-commerce stores. This removal of intermediaries, like department stores, between producers and consumers not only streamlines the sales process but also provides a marketing environment in which individual brands can shine. Among the advantages are:

—The brand can establish connectivity directly with the consumer without relying on a retailer to generate visibility and traffic.

—The brand can own its consumer data and establish its own policies with regard to customer service and returns.

—The brand can set the product slate and decide when to introduce new products.

—The brand will not be lost in a group of like brands.

—The brand does not have to share revenue with intermediaries.

The upshot is brands that are typically limited to department store or showroom settings in the US can flourish in China through e-commerce. In the US, Kohler products are typically found in a Home Depot setting. In China, the Kohler flagship e-commerce store saw 50 per cent growth last year. L'Oréal products are generally found in grocery stores and pharmacies in America. In China, sales on L'Oréal's flagship e-commerce site have almost doubled over the past three years. Recognizing how well single-brand stores do in China, L'Oréal also opened a flagship e-commerce store for Lancôme, a makeup and skincare line that has generally been limited to US department or beauty stores.

E-commerce poses challenges to multi-brand retailers, but some do quite well online. For example, one would not go to a fiction store or a merlot store but would go to a bookstore or a wine store, where a variety of options aids decision-making. Bibliophiles and oenophiles seem to be happier in a collective setting where they can explore as much as shop. Auto supply stores tell us the same principle applies to the gear-heads.

Retail consultant Lionel Binnie says that the two fundamental aspects of the buyer's journey are discovery and fulfilment. E-commerce makes fulfilment very convenient but physical retail helps many people in the discovery process, particularly with what he describes as 'heterogeneous shopping products' and 'unsought products.' You might go to the hardware store to get some nails, but you might also return with an electronic level. Or you might go to the supermarket to purchase vegetables for your lamb stew, but you might pick up peanut brittle in the checkout line. In my view, although this is accurate it becomes less important as digital stores improve their artificial intelligence and consumer behavior becomes increasingly digitally oriented.[*]

Indeed, beyond a few examples, it seems that Chinese consumers are more comfortable purchasing from single-brand stores because they are able to easily find the precise product they desire. Companies that are willing to make an effort to reach these consumers find that they can directly engage with hundreds of millions of active buyers. There are initial costs and complexities, but eliminating the intermediate levels of distributors, wholesalers, and retailers can bring increased returns to the foreign brand and pave a path to long-term success in the market.

---

[*] https://msourceideas.com/a-model-for-predicting-on-line-vs-off-line-consumer-shopping-behavior/

How to Avoid the Mistake of Nothing Different

Once you start in China, think of yourself as a rookie again. You're a new product in the market. You no longer have word of mouth, brand awareness, or a social media following. It's like you landed on a distant planet. Nobody's heard of you. Nobody loves you. Yet. You need to behave like a start-up.

You can avoid the Mistake of Nothing Different with a little market research. How big is your market segment in China? Who are your competitors in the market? In what ways might your customer base be different? This will show you how to adapt your model to the new market.

There are several avenues to pursue market research:

—Reports and studies from market research firms such as Forrester and Gartner.

—Trade associations and business groups: the British Chamber of Commerce Shanghai; or the US-China Business Council; as well as sectoral organizations in segments such as fashion or cosmetics.

—Library research and government bodies: you can study economic trends and consumer developments through the *Wall Street Journal*; and market studies from the US Department of Commerce.

—Contract with an e-commerce agency or ad agency. A China market research firm can evaluate what your competitors are doing in China. Where are they selling online? What is their monthly revenue? How does their selection and pricing compare to their home market? What social media platforms are they on? Modesty requires me to note that beyond Export Now there are many other research firms such as China Market Research Group.

—Your own field research. If you visit a few shopping malls in Shanghai, you can determine what products are being sold, and the average price. If you look online you can see who is selling what products at what price.

You don't need to mimic what other brands are doing, but at least try to understand their behavior and their rationale. Some of it might well apply to your brand.

Secrets of the multi-market brand. When to break from MOTS.

If your company is active in several markets, you have already learned some lessons that will boost your chances for success in China. To be sure, companies that are going to China as their first international move still have every chance of success but will not have prior international experience to draw on. This is a lesson I learned when I led market entry programs at the US Department of Commerce: companies that were operating in many markets tended to do better than those that had a presence only in their home market, but this had more to do with the international journey rather than the additional revenue.

The process of going international forced a company to adapt to each new market. As a result, the international firm became a learning organization which encompassed several different successful models, and the lessons from each new market could be applied in other markets. The international company tended to develop a feedback mechanism and process improvements more readily than the purely domestic company.

Indeed, if you ask the leadership of many firms what they want to do tomorrow, you are likely to hear that they want to do tomorrow what they did yesterday. MOTS lives.

In other words, many business people (like all of us) have a preference for the familiar. We all follow patterns of behavior and we like to stay in our comfort zone. I see this regularly when I discuss China opportunities. We will have a nice conversation with a successful mid-size company, but unless it has an international culture it will have an overwhelming focus on building out a successful domestic model.

The management philosophy at these firms tends to be:

—Reliant on the organic growth that has served them well over the years;

—Task-driven organizations, with people looking at monthly and quarterly results; and

—Heavily product-focused.

These companies tend to dominate their space or be a segment leader. All of this means these companies have a strong incentive not to diverge from their current set of activities, and not to think about what changes might be in order. MOTS is the key principle at these firms. They do the same set of activities as they did last year.

More revenue, more customers, more market share, more net is a common-sense approach, but it is not a strategy—it is a behavior pattern. It is a tendency of doing what the company has always done, presumably because it has more or less always worked. This approach makes sense if the world is static. If the world is standing still, if technology is standing still, and if competitors are standing still, it is okay if the business stands still as well. But there are moving pieces out there, so you had better move as well. Unless the business incorporates a bit of a change culture, it will fall behind. Therefore, some sort of strategy is in order.

Define Strategy

Strategy means a break with MOTS. It means the business can allocate resources without the normal formula for a return, which allows for experimentation. Strategy can mean you are doing something different, and the constituency for this change has not yet been established. Strategy can mean a course, the immediate benefit of which is not self-evident. With any new project, the immediate costs are clear and the benefits are uncertain.

Strategy can mean a journey into the unknown. You are taking steps that require you to stretch beyond current capabilities. A new product launch, or a new sales channel, or a new market could each be an element of a strategy

For most companies, the decision to go into a new market is a matter of strategy, because growth is no longer just MOTS. The best expression of this might be a decision to go to China. On any given day it might not make sense to think about what you could do differently. It could make sense to only do what you did yesterday, but cumulatively, this could lead to a disaster.

The companies that fail in China are those that jump in without incorporating it in a strategy. They usually posit something like: *I am going to show up in China, start selling, and increase my ad spend as revenue grows. End of story.*

Just showing up is not a strategy. Just showing up is what you do if you don't have a strategy.

> ### Key Takeaways
>
> ➤ The most common business mistake in China is the *Mistake of Nothing Different*.
> ➤ If you want to avoid this mistake, you need to be able to adapt, which means controlled experimentation using analytical tools and feedback.
> ➤ Companies that cannot adapt can only use a More Of The Same approach. Those that can adapt and experiment can adopt a strategy to win.

5

Your China Strategy

The Main Adjustment is that You Need to Adjust

Foreign consumer brands are still popular in China because consumers know that they will get the quality they expect. But Chinese brands are moving up quickly so the foreign brands have to be flexible and inventive to tailor their products to Chinese tastes and desires.

—in conversation with Jim McGregor,
Chairman APCO Worldwide, Greater China

How versatile are you? If your company, your brand, your marketing department, your finance team are inflexible, then China—or any overseas market—might not work for you.

In this chapter, we go beyond the *Mistake of Nothing Different* to discuss how new market entry, and China market entry in particular, has implications for your entire company. We will explore how your company can move away from a MOTS approach and develop a strategy specifically for China.

There are a few simple reasons why foreign companies get frustrated in China:

—The Finance Department is unhappy. You have to invest to build the brand. You will likely encounter a worse return on investment (ROI) in China than in your home market because you are not yet at scale and it can take a while to refine your message. Also, the payment cycle can deteriorate. Shipping and customs clearance can easily add a few weeks to logistics, so you need to offer a distributor 60-day terms, not 30.

—The Marketing Department is unhappy. They have to develop a brand narrative beyond what they might do in your home market. You are actively courting the Chinese consumer in a way you do not have to in your home market.

—The CEO is unhappy. Sales and profits will not be linear for the first few years. It might take one or two years to build your brand and start to get sales to your desired level. You have to be able to experiment. It takes time to learn and adjust. Things can go wrong.

Because of this unhappiness, you need to first build an internal consensus on goals, a commitment of resources, and an eye on the long game before you get to China. You have to agree that you can't use your home market metrics to evaluate your China success.

'Call Me When China Stops Being Weird'

Even though they understand the potential of the market, companies often hesitate to pursue a China entry strategy—put off by the complexity, costs and challenges of the market.

During a generally pleasant lunch, one CEO summed up his concern with a pithy bit of sarcasm: 'Call me when China stops being weird.' In other words, there are differences in China in terms of strategy, timing, costs and expertise compared to selling in their domestic market.

If the company cannot deal with these differences, then it's not China that's 'weird'. In some respects, this is not a China point as much as a broader new market point. Every market in the world will have distinctive attributes—this means a different cost structure, a learning curve and a delayed ROI as a brand builds.

And beyond the general international points, there are China-specific challenges. When it comes to China e-commerce, *different* is a much better word than *weird*.

Many companies that can properly boast of international success primarily found that success in Europe or Canada, markets that have many similarities with the US market. China might be the first major market they encounter that has meaningful differences. Differences in culture, language, purchasing power, and consumer preferences all mean that international brands have to learn and adjust. It is the largest market in the world, so it might take more than six or twelve months before a brand gains meaningful traction.

The Revenge of the J-Curve—The Downside Model

One of the differences between results in China and results in the home market, is that the China results are frequently in the form of a J-curve. The J-curve plots the results we typically see with business initiatives from new product launches to new market entry. As with the letter 'J,' the curve first goes down and then rebounds. In other words, if you choose to enter a new market—or launch a new product—you might lose money at first. Over time, as your marketing efficiency and operations improve, the venture turns profitable.

Can you avoid the J-curve? Sure. You can avoid all risks and all costs by never innovating and keeping all of your activity domestic. If you never experiment, if you never launch a new product, if you never enter a new market, you can indeed avoid the J-curve.

If you have to choose between a $1,00,000 order from a department store chain in your home market or $1,00,000 in sales in China's e-commerce market, the cash from the home market customer seems a lot sweeter. You have established payment terms, there's no need to invest in advertising, and logistics are predictable.

This is the paradox: on any given day, your returns will be better if you simply stick to your home market, but over the long run, your returns will be better if you go to China. Of course, the moment you begin operating in China, your margins drop, your efficiencies drop, the level of clarity drops and your frustration might build.

So China is best treated as a long-term initiative. It will take time to develop your market. It could take a few months just to hit your stride, iron out logistics, determine your core product slate and replenish inventory at the right pace. China is a journey, and it is not for everybody. But for brands that are serious about innovation and growth, it's time to start. The weird ones, it might turn out, are those who will not go beyond their home market.

SKUs and Pricing

As another example of business decisions that will likely be different from the home market, every company has to grapple with the twin questions of SKUs (stock-keeping units) and pricing when it enters the China market. Each question embodies trade-offs

With SKUs: If you opt for larger inventory, your sales will be higher and you will understand the market more quickly, but you will have to absorb the costs of financing that larger inventory and some of it might be slow-moving. My view is you want to build out your initial inventory profile based on the following considerations:

—If your model is cross-border, as will be discussed in Chapter 8, you can fill your orders initially from your main inventory pool. Thus, you have no additional inventory carrying costs. This will give you the opportunity to understand demand. An apparel company, for example, will note that size and color preferences will be different in China than in western markets and there will likely be other differences as well.

We worked with a company that wanted to introduce a health supplement into China. Our research showed that a competitor was already in the market with the same supplement and doing well, but they were only selling the product as a solid pill. Our client decided to enter the market with a supplement in liquid form. Thus, we were able to gain market share and establish the brand in China while avoiding direct competition with the established leader:

—As you move inventory to a Free Trade Zone or in-country, you will be establishing a new inventory pool and you will need to understand the costs and benefits of different inventory models.

—In general, you should have an inventory that can satisfy 98–99 per cent of market demand, and the remaining 1–2 per cent will have to order from your home market store or rely on daigous. 'Daigous' are the individual buyers that informally purchase goods overseas to resell in China. This constitutes a grey market in China in which the merchants are not authorized but the goods are genuine.

—If you are launching with an in-country model, the cost of inventory goes up again because it has to be labelled for China and can only be re-exported with difficulty. My advice is to start with as narrow an inventory selection as you can while still fully populating the store. You can project demand based on what you learned while running a cross-border store and you can also see what competitors in China are doing.

With pricing: You will find the price to consumers in China will typically be higher than in your home market, due to several factors: extra logistics costs, an operation that is not yet at scale, and for goods that are deemed to be luxury, a 22 per cent VAT (value-added tax).

You have to decide whether to price your goods consistent with your home market price, in which case you will forgo some of your profit margin, or whether to mark up your products a bit to account for these extra costs. You probably will not be able to raise your prices sufficiently to completely offset the additional costs.

If the Chinese customers sense you have raised prices unreasonably, they will make it known on social media. Remember, Chinese consumers can make use of daigous or they can purchase directly from US e-commerce sites.

Why the China Country Manager Gets No Love from its Head Office

All of these changes and adaptations for China that we have been discussing in this chapter can also have implications for internal management and communications. As a foreign business country manager in China, your relations with your China team will tend to be manageable and positive, but your relations with your own head office might be strained.

We all know that China is the fastest growing of the major markets. Companies readily concede that they cannot become truly global unless they have a China strategy. Why is it, then, that the head offices of many companies seem so averse to China?

The China results might seem weaker than original plans. The folks back home don't want to talk about it. They don't want to think through any China initiatives. And whatever you do, do not pitch for extra resources for China. There is simply no appetite at the head office. The China country manager gets no love.

Let me explain this apparent contradiction in China's importance to the company and its role in corporate planning, and offer some solutions as well.

The China Contradiction

1.   A mismatch between macro expectations and micro results.

At a macro level, China is indeed a land of superlatives: biggest *this*, largest *that*, fastest-growing *something else*. This *Law of Scale* was the central theme of Chapter 2. This size whets our appetite and implies that somehow 1·4 billion Chinese will each purchase one item from us. However, the micro results can be very different from expectations. It is not unusual to find a $500 million foreign apparel company with $1–2 million of sales in China. Instead of seeing this as a nice toe in the water, the head office will frequently view these numbers with a groan.

2.   China is . . . different.

Not worse, but just by being different the company is required to go through a process of learning and adapting that might be a challenge. Particularly for companies that have only done business in Western markets, coming to terms with different procedures for shipping, labelling, and product testing can be a headache. This extra heartburn combined with the micro mismatch above can quickly sour a company to the market. The cost-benefit curve moves the wrong way. Whose idea was this, anyhow?

3. The CNN effect.

Global digital news brings the world to us in ways that can be disconcerting. Almost by definition, bad news travels faster than good. And with 20 per cent of the world's population, China has at least 20 per cent of the world's problems. Not a day goes by that we do not hear about some sort of potential disruption in the market, be it an economic slowdown, foreign policy issues, or intellectual property problems. This is not to argue that these are not serious issues, but it is to argue that regardless of their importance they tend to have little to no impact on the consumer market. After all, among the greatest political shocks in the world recently was the Brexit vote in the UK and the presidential election in the US, neither of which had material impact on consumer activity. Nonetheless, the CNN effect means that at some point this year, your head office will be hearing about something amiss in China, and questioning whether that will impact their China plans.

Three Solutions

1. Maybe the problem is not China, it is you.

If your company is evaluating China as it evaluates developed markets, it is bound to fixate on the macro-micro mismatch. Companies need to develop a different set of metrics for developing markets and calibrate that approach as well. For example, if sales in China are only 10 per cent of sales in Canada, can the company put together a structure so that the resource allocation for China is commensurate? You will want to localize your key performance indicators (KPIs).

Companies that can calibrate activity proportionate to the market will be happy in China. Companies that are cookie-cutters will be disappointed. Remember, most of the revenue for multinationals takes place in the developed world. China is the outlier. When a company says it has a China problem, it frequently means it has a developing-market problem or a non-Western problem.

How to Localize your KPIs

It is a bit unfair to the China team to expect the same margins when sales are not yet at scale, or to expect the same advertising efficiencies when the brand is new to market. You might want to use different Key Performance Indicators in China than in your home market, at least for the first 12 months or so. A few suggestions:

—How do your ratings and reviews track compared to competition?
—Are you seeing steady growth in Unique Visitors (UV) to your e-commerce store?
—Is there a steady increase in followers on social media?
—Are sales increasing? (this is unlikely to reflect straight-line growth because of the importance of promotions and holidays).

2. View adjustments as Capital Expenditure.

You are building a new team with new procedures. These are capital expenditure (CAPEX) requirements that you will not find in other markets, at least not in the same way. You won't have the same numbers in China or the same ratios. You need some capacity for new market experimentation. Alibaba President Michael Evans shared a similar sentiment when we discussed this challenge of dealing with corporate decision-making regarding China: 'You are battling for mindshare, battling pre-conceived notions of China.'[*]

3. E-commerce does not augment the strategy; it is the strategy.

Nothing gets you in the market with lower cost and lower risk than e-commerce. The cost of opening an online store might easily be one-

---

[*] https://www.forbes.com/sites/franklavin/2017/02/23/why-the-china-country-manager-gets-no-love-from-its-head-office/?sh=26c565e3f62b

tenth the cost of a physical store. So if you want to calibrate resources to market opportunity, e-commerce is your best bet.

The bottom line: In the long-run China e-commerce is an upside model, but in the short-run it is a downside model. In other words, the long-run benefit of e-commerce is that it allows you greater revenue, but the short-run benefit of e-commerce is that it limits your costs and exposure.

Not a bad point to make to those folks at the head office.

L'Oréal Case Study

L'Oréal is a nice example of ongoing adaptation and experimentation in China, to push its e-commerce results as far as possible. This world-renowned, French brand has long enjoyed success in China, but it has had particularly strong results in China e-commerce, growing ten-fold in that channel since 2011. Not only is e-commerce the fastest growing channel for L'Oréal in China, by 2020 it accounted for 50 per cent of L'Oréal's China sales.[*]

Recently, L'Oréal started moving into 'new retail' which combines offline and online channels. 'New retail' also encompasses augmented reality, virtual reality, and artificial intelligence.

Today L'Oréal in China uses artificial intelligence to provide skincare diagnostics for its Vichy brand on Tmall.

Similarly, L'Oréal uses augmented reality to promote personalization and co-branding. L'Oréal uses AR to let people 'try on' lipstick simply by pointing their smartphone camera at themselves. Why try on two colors of lipstick when AR can let you try on twenty? L'Oréal's Giorgio Armani brand became the first luxury line to use this technology on WeChat. WeChat users can order them from Giorgio Armani Beauty's mini-app shopping site.

The use of AI and AR boosted L'Oréal's already-successful, online-to-offline model and its social networks promotion strategy, helping the brand stay tech-oriented and relevant to younger shoppers.

---

[*] https://www.shine.cn/biz/company/2003053516/

Key Takeaways

➤ Your model needs to be adjusted for China. Build consensus with the head office. Do not go to China with the goal of implementing the home market strategy.

➤ Your results are likely to be a J-curve. China is a journey. Don't expect instant success. There has to be some appetite for investment and some sort of time horizon. A company might be over one hundred years old in its home market, yet some in leadership might expect China results in twelve months.

➤ New markets require different metrics than mature markets. Coca Cola has been investing in China for forty years and still probably only reaches 90 per cent of the population.

6

From a Product to a Brand

The work of an advertising agency is warmly and immediately human. It deals with human needs, wants, dreams and hopes. Its 'product' cannot be turned out on an assembly line.[*]

——Leo Burnett

Brands need to be proactively telling their stories in this era of consumer consciousness and to establish two-ways communications with Chinese consumers while doing so. Discovery has become a very important part of the consumer journey, and Chinese consumers want to know the backstories and what brands stand for. They want to be inspired and delighted, and to feel like part of a movement.

—Man-Chung Cheung, Insider Intelligence

Are you selling ballpoint pens? Office staplers? Fish hooks?

I hope not, because anything purely functional or mass-produced can usually be manufactured for less in China and you will have trouble competing.

To compete in China, your product not only has to be worthy, you must also be able to articulate your brand's identity and message. You must ask yourself questions on three topics:

---

[*] https://www.brandingstrategyinsider.com/the-advertising-wisdom-of-leo-burnett/#. YKALfqhKg2w

- **The product**: What makes a product worthy? What is distinctive about your product? What does your product do that no other product does? Or are you simply viewed as functional?
- **The emotional content**: What does your product stand for? Beyond the distinctiveness of the product, how does it make your customers feel? Consumers who feel happy about a purchase will share that happiness. Since your brand will be deeper into the premium space in China than in your home market, customers in China might take a pass on any premium product that doesn't make them feel comfortable, aspirational, cooler, or better.
- **The social strength**: Do people talk about your product or seek it out? Is it a successful brand? Do people ask for it by name?

Smart brand managers deal with these questions every day, but you will have to deal with them anew in China where the answers might be different than in your home market. Don't make the *Mistake of Nothing Different* when it comes to brand definition.

This chapter will provide a more in-depth look at how businesses can make the transition to becoming a proper brand. So how do you undertake the brand journey?

Long Live Your Brand

Consumer brands face an array of challenges. A global study for the Reputation Institute, a management consultancy, showed that just 48 per cent of consumers polled said that, 'brands appear genuine about what they say and stand for,' down from 64 per cent a year ago. Additionally, only 47 per cent felt that brands stand out from the crowd, also down from the previous year's 61 per cent.[*]

But the dominant brands face a challenge. Generic brands and niche brands are helping segment consumer brands, and e-commerce is their weapon of choice. This trend of insurgent brands carving up the market share traditionally held by more established brands is perhaps most pronounced in China.

---

[*] https://www.reptrak.com/blog/2020-global-reptrak-study-executive-summary/

Think about Procter and Gamble. P&G's genius is all about scale and scope. They find the middle of the bell curve of consumer demand and they take advantage of that position through scale. No one can match their volume and distribution acumen, so they dominate shelf space, chain relationships and replenishment cycles. That volume gives them considerable unit cost advantages as well. P&G is King Kong.

But e-commerce changes these rules. Scale no longer carries the same advantages. Online, a $20 million toothpaste brand can have as much 'shelf space' as a $1 billion brand. The incumbent's defensive power is diminished. The $20 million brand might be more experimental in new product launches and perhaps more audacious in its advertising.

Similarly, local competitors can start chewing away from below. The value consumer is up for grabs. The local brand will tend to have a lower cost structure than P&G, and Chinese companies tend to be less sensitive to ROI than US brands. This might be a long-term financial weakness, but it is a short-term benefit to market share. China-based Yunnan Baiyao brand has already passed Crest and the other foreign brands to emerge as the leading toothpaste in the market.[*]

Another problem for P&G: the mega-brands have to play defense. If you are in the middle of the bell curve, you have to be everything to everybody. The insurgent brands and the niche brands can play to a narrow appeal. There is nothing wrong with a strategy to go from 1 per cent to 2 per cent market share if the market is China.

We are moving from a Budweiser world to a craft beer world, but why? What is wrong with the established brands? Here are five drivers of this trend:

- Consumers are more educated and more empowered than ever before.
- People want to express individuality, not conformity, so the incumbent brand can be less appealing.
- Consumers are curious and they like to experiment. Brand loyalty means a lack of curiosity, a lack of imagination, and a failure to believe in better possibilities.

---

[*] https://www.ibisworld.com/china/market-research-reports/toothpaste-toothbrush-manufacturing-industry/

- Mass prosperity means that mass brands are less distinctive.
- Nobody wants what their mom and dad wanted. This is one of the rare moments in human history where we have consecutive generations of consumer affluence. Each generation has an impulse to define their own preferences. The quest for novelty and identity becomes important.

The decline of traditional brands opens up opportunities for new brands. A White House study reported that

> . . . the variety of imported goods increased approximately three-fold between 1972 and 2001.

Retail expert Kathleen Kusek explains,

> The standard for brand switching is no longer the failure of a brand to perform but rather its inability to seem like an entirely new and interesting option . . .*

Moreover, technology and social media have made it easier for a brand to position itself as new and interesting.

How do these insurgent brands win market share? Again, four reasons:

First, they talk to people. A good brand needs to have a conversation. Traditional communication meant the brand defined itself to the consumer through advertising. Today, consumers define the brand through social media and the brand is one more participant in that conversation.

Second, they talk about the world beyond the brand. Consumers see the product as a means to an end, an opportunity for a better life. Do not just talk about the product, talk about what the product enables you to do and how it makes you feel.

Third, they're nimble with digital and creative with campaigns. Traditional brands had a TV spot and a full-page Sunday newspaper ad. Today's brands are all over digital and social platforms, allowing for a

---

* https://www.forbes.com/sites/kathleenkusek/2016/07/25/the-death-of-brand-loyalty-cultural-shifts-mean-its-gone-forever/

targeted, powerful message. Digital communications can describe how to use the product, demonstrate different applications, even discuss whether the product is green or organic.

Fourth, they have a model that allows for success with a small market share. Traditional brands used market leadership to drive production and based success on low cost and mass distribution. If your brand will occupy only a small percentage of the market—common for international brands in China—you need a cost structure that allows you to be profitable at lower levels of sales.

As we migrate from a mass-market world to a segmented world, we see this trend most pronouncedly in China, because of both the size of the market and the paucity of historical brands. Remember, Chinese consumers are perhaps the most sophisticated in the world, but this is a trend that has emerged only in recent decades. The legacy brands don't have much of a legacy. The dominant brands aren't all that dominant. There is still considerable opportunity in the market. What should brands do?

Experiment with brand extensions: Better to cannibalize yourself with new products and varieties than to let others cannibalize you. Consumer expert Kaleigh Moore notes that luggage company Away is moving into accessories and apparel and Offspring Beauty has moved into skin care.[*] Marketing superstar Tom Doctoroff tells us personal care brands in China are more likely to be full spectrum. The soap company will also manufacture shampoo, skin lotion, and even a mouthwash all under the same brand.[†]

Heavy digital experimentation: Play around with niche groups and niche messaging. You can market mosquito repellent to beachgoers, adventure trekkers, as well as new moms—and each of these groups have their own chat rooms, web sites, and affinity groups.

---

[*] https://www.forbes.com/sites/kaleighmoore/2019/05/23/consumer-brands-are-leaning-into-product-line-expansion/?sh=543a8682348e

[†] http://www.tomdoctoroff.com/thought-leadership/

Refresh what's great: Look at how long-term successes like Nike (forty-nine years old) and Levi's (168 years old) keep their brands fresh. They are able to comfortably speak to younger consumers by continually updating images, models, and even music. Consumers gravitate to established brands not because they are venerable, but because they continually renew themselves.

New market entry strategy: As we have related earlier in this book, the best defense is a good offense. Don't allocate all your resources to your home market.

Luxury E-Commerce

Of all the market segments that e-commerce has forced to think anew about strategy, luxury is perhaps the most significant. Conventional thinking holds that e-commerce might work fine for everyday consumer products or groceries, but it would not be a successful channel for luxury goods. The argument is that a successful luxury brand depends on exclusivity and e-commerce stands for the opposite—universal accessibility. How could the luxury culture, born in the salons of Paris and the fashion shows of Milan, square with the one-click culture of e-commerce?

Yet the China experience has thrown that conventional wisdom into the trash. Beyond the moves in fashion, JD introduced its 'White Glove' delivery service, adding a high-end concierge dimension to its luxury offering. It invested $400 million in global luxury retailer Farfetch, with whom it will open a joint platform.[*] In turn, Tmall launched its Luxury Pavilion; and JD fired back by launching a luxury watch channel. And a number of luxury-only sites have flourished, such as Secoo.com. There are other verticals that are fashion pure-plays, such as Mei.com, Farfetch, and Net-a-Porter. What's going on?

---

[*] https://ir.jd.com/news-releases/news-release-details/jdcom-and-farfetch-partner-open-ultimate-gateway-bringing-luxury

First, e-commerce continues to gain consumer acceptance. Whereas twenty years ago it was only a place to buy books, and fifteen years ago you could bank online, today consumers are comfortable with a range of online purchases from educational services to luxury products. Porsche and Cadillac joined the 2020 Singles' Day sales, not afraid for their luxury image to be associated with a major promotional event.[*] No surprise that luxury items would over time gain online acceptance and no surprise that China leads the way. According to Bain, China is the region with the highest annual luxury growth rate, boasting a 45 per cent jump in sales.[†]

Second, the luxury brands saw an opening. Remember there are distinct advantages to e-commerce, as well as possible disadvantages. E-commerce allows the brand to know the customer and capture customer information. High-value customers can be cultivated with curated offerings. Events can be managed through customer history. Cross-sell and renewal activity are now possible. Louis Vuitton will attach a high value to knowing which customers buy a new bag annually. Secoo worked with Tencent to create profiles of its 15 million customers.

Third, the e-commerce model can be adjusted. Luxury brands can harvest the upside of e-commerce and guard against the potential downside. Exclusivity is balanced against universality. A brand can have a store on Tmall for the general public and it can also have a store on the Tmall Luxury Pavilion, where consumers may only participate through invitation. Tmall and JD are setting up a ladder of activity. At the base is the traditional open platform similar to Amazon in the US. Up a step is an exclusive platform, which is invitation-only. It is a little like a bank offering retail service to anyone with an account, and once that account reaches

---

[*] http://epaper.chinadaily.com.cn/a/202011/16/WS5fb1c966a31099a234351c91. html#:~:text=More%20than%2050%20auto%20brands,the%20country%2C%20 according%20to%20Tmall.

[†] https://www.bain.com/about/media-center/press-releases/2020/covid_19_crisis_ pushes_luxury_to_sharpest_fall_ever_but_catalyses_industrys_ability_to_transform/

a certain threshold of activity, the customer will be directed to the private bank.

What does this mean for luxury brands?

1. *You need an e-commerce strategy*: A toe-in-the-water approach is a good way to start. Use a slimmed-down product slate. Do not attempt to replicate your offline experience online, at least to start.

2. *Maintain exclusivity*: Keep certain products off the e-commerce channel. Go light on merchandising, heavy on lifestyle tips. Remember, your customers are not buying a product as much as they are joining a club.

3. *Integrate your channels—online to offline*: Use a customer management system that recognizes the online shopper when they make an in-store purchase. Increase the number of events. Think of lifestyle events, rather than merchandising—an accessory brand might host an evening wine-tasting, or a watch brand may host a stock-market discussion.

A Word of Caution on Results

As you start to experiment and learn in China, one of the more common questions you will encounter will be how to model the success of a product in the market. Will your product work or not, and to what extent?

There are probably several valid approaches to answer this, but there's also a potential problem with one of them. The flawed methodological approach I see frequently when discussing prospects for a brand in China e-commerce is typically something like this: A certain category is 'X' large or growing at 'Y' per cent, therefore China is an attractive market for your product. So, we will hear that dairy is a $26 billion market* or oral care is a

---

* https://www.dairyreporter.com/Article/2020/09/29/Covid-19-to-add-extra-1.6bn-to-milk-sales-in-China-in-2020

$5.4 billion market[*] in China. Therefore, the faulty argument goes, China is a good market for dairy or oral care products.

But the logic is faulty for at least three reasons: the competitive map, brand strength and Say's Law.

Competitive Map: Can't See the Forest for the Trees

When you look at competition, the success of a category probably has little to do with your brand's ultimate success in the market. It might make sense to keep away from the middle of the bell curve—where the market is strongest—because that is likely where competition will also be strongest. What matters more than the strength of the category is the overall competitive map.

What if you produce shampoos, and the most popular scented shampoo is strawberry, accounting for 30 per cent of the market. Lime shampoo, on the other hand, accounts for 3 per cent of the market. So strawberry is what you launch, right?

Not so fast. First, take a look at the competitive map. Every shampoo producer sees the same data you do, so you may well face a problem if you simply follow the herd. While the lime shampoo market segment is one-tenth the size, that also means competition could be tamer. Remember, your brand will be deeper into the premium space in China than you are in your home market. It might make sense to play for the edges of the bell curve, rather than the middle.

Brand Strength: Are You a Leader or a Follower?

Brand strength is the second reason. Are you following the market or are you shaping it? If you are a strong premium product, you are shaping the market. Consumers seek you out, and they will insist on your particular brand. If you are more of a commodity product, you're following the market. Many consumers might not know who you are, but you represent good value for money, so they are comfortable with your offering. This

---

[*] https://www.statista.com/outlook/70060000/117/oral-care/china

does not mean your logic or your strategy is faulty, but it does mean you are likely to have less market power to shape outcomes.

One key test here is social media. If consumers want to discuss your product and want a conversation with your brand, you have a strong brand. If they are indifferent to your brand and don't discuss it on social media, chances are you're considered more of a commodity.

Say's Law: Who decided China likes pizzas?

The somewhat-related third reason is there is a little Say's Law in every brand. Named after the French economist Jean-Baptiste Say, this law of economics holds that supply creates its own demand. It's not always true, but there's probably some truth in it for every successful brand.

For example, Procter and Gamble did not wait for consumers to write asking for mint or lemon-flavored toothpaste. They introduced them into the Crest brand family, to roaring success. The supply of the product induced demand. Some consumers have a penchant for experimentation, and many of us are willing to be educated.

The best recent example in China might be pizza. There was not much in the way of intrinsic demand for pizza when Pizza Hut entered China in 1990. People were unfamiliar with the product and it was not readily available. The pizza restaurant chains had to create demand. Pizza Hut modified its menu to use less cheese and tomato sauce, two ingredients that are not naturally part of the Chinese diet. They overspent on ads as compared to their home market. And they had the discipline to build slowly. Today Pizza Hut has 2000 restaurants in China[*] and pizza consumption is projected to grow at 12 per cent annually through 2028.[†] Pizza Hut understood the *Law of Convergence* and also had the marketing acumen to make it work.

So maybe the lack of demand for lime shampoo reflects as much that there are many more suppliers selling strawberry and pushing that market segment.

---

[*] https://edition.cnn.com/2019/03/05/business/kfc-fastfood-pizza-hut-china/index.html

[†] https://www.businesswire.com/news/home/20200106005513/en/Chinas-Demand-for-Pizzas-will-Continue-to-Grow-at-12-by-2028---ResearchAndMarkets.com

Sure, look at category trends. But remember, if you're a premium brand, you have the capability to shape those trends. If you are a mass brand you are more likely riding the wave.

Evaluate the competitive map, measure the strength of your brand, and remember Say's Law.

In China it is not as important to compete in the largest market segment as it is to dominate the market segment in which you compete.

Key Takeaways

> You need to define your brand again for Chinese consumers. You are trying to recreate the same brand potency in a new market that took a lifetime to establish in your home market.

> The competitive map in China will likely be different; you are unlikely to enjoy the scale or scope of your home market.

> The intangible elements of your brand, such as the emotional content, might be more important than the tangible elements.

Section Two

Starting to Jog—for people who are thinking about a China strategy

7

How to Court the Chinese Consumer

At times it appears that e-commerce is becoming the only commerce in China. In our offices in Shanghai and Beijing, couriers are in and out of the office all day bringing everything from food to clothing to household goods that my colleagues order online. The pandemic has only accelerated online shopping. Older people who previously resisted online purchasing adapted and learned and may likely not go back to predominantly shopping in person.

—in conversation with Jim McGregor,
Chairman APCO Worldwide, Greater China

I had to launch a leading American food brand in China, for a product that every home in the United States knows and cherishes: peanut butter. But in China, no one normally uses peanut butter; nobody normally eats peanut butter and jelly sandwiches. Although the popularity of sandwiches continues to grow, they are not a regular part of the diet in China. And what is peanut butter to the Chinese consumer? Is it a health food? A convenience food? Is it a good bargain? Are the moms who make their kids peanut butter sandwiches good moms, lazy moms, experimental moms or what? Courting the consumer is a journey.

We first examined the brand's relationship with the Chinese consumer in Chapter 3—the *Law of Convergence*—in which we postulated that, in general, Chinese consumers will be similar to consumers in other markets at similar levels of income. That's a good starting point, but what are

65

the differences? In what ways might Chinese consumers be different from consumers in other markets?

In this chapter, we look at these differences that determine consumer behavior; we get to know the Chinese consumer, including the Post-Millennial Generation; and we discover what interests them.

Here is what we have learned so far about drivers of consumer behavior in China:

1. Consumers are digital. And by 'digital' I mean they are on their smartphones. The phone is where they connect with friends, get their news, share their stories, pursue friendship and romance, play games, or watch their favorite movies.
2. Consumers are social. Chinese consumers follow the social dimension of the brand more than western consumers. They are sensitive to ratings and reviews. Smart brands emphasize review management, carefully following the reviews and quickly adjusting for any patterns or complaints. One brand we worked with was so sensitive to potential social criticism that it sent a note of apology and a small gift (a box of raisins) in response to complaints.
3. Consumers are courted. China might be the world's most competitive consumer market. Every day, brands are connecting with consumers, telling their story, explaining their value proposition, launching engagement strategies such as games or promotions. The consumer wants to feel special, important, sought after. You will have to do more, say more, imagine more, and (dare I say it?) spend more in China than you will in other markets.

We sometimes forget this responsibility to court precisely because it is so embedded in our culture and actions in our home market. This is what you have done all along—and continue doing, back home—but you have the entire life of the company to build a following, so you are the incumbent. You enjoy a good reputation and a satisfied customer base. All of those strengths wash out when you enter a new market. Every brand becomes peanut butter.

Particularly when the new market brings with it different languages and cultures, there might be little to no familiarity with your product and there are a special set of social and cultural factors that drive spending. There is something new or distinctive about the brand but the Chinese consumer might not immediately warm to it. You have your journey as well.

What Factors Drive Consumer Spending?

We know that China is the largest and fastest-growing consumer market in the world. What is less well understood are the forces that shape Chinese consumerism. To what extent is it the need for a product and to what extent might it be self-indulgence or materialism? In what ways would those consumer patterns in China be different from those in the West?

In my view there are larger social and cultural factors at play that drive consumer spending:

1. **Consumerism as a statement of individualism**: To have a choice means to have consumer choice. You are what you consume. Consumption is an expression of self. It allows you to explore the world through its products, to experiment with lifestyle choices, and to do so safely and anonymously. You might never get to France, but you can try French wine. California might be intimidating, but you can go to Shanghai Disneyland. Remember, China is only one generation out of poverty. Indeed, the enthusiasm for choice is reflected in the enthusiasm Chinese consumers have for online shopping—the country's giant shopping websites, Tmall, Taobao and JD, offer more than a billion listings for products from mom-and-pop Chinese retailers to the largest multinational consumer electronics brands.

2. **Consumerism is a statement of success**: American economist Thorstein Veblen popularized the concept of 'conspicuous consumption.' When consumption is no longer driven solely by need, it becomes a way of making a statement that you have disposable income, and you can—at least in certain respects—enjoy life on your terms. Simple pleasures—a pair of Nikes, a smartphone, chic apparel—become statements of personal identity. Why is this pattern strongest among younger consumers? They are the ones sending and

receiving 'market signals'. The biggest singles' bar in the world is the sidewalks of Shanghai. If you are going for a stroll, might as well wear your finest.

3. **The triumph of me-ism**: Me-ism is not the same as selfishness, it is self-directed activity. The one-child policy means most Chinese do not have siblings, aunts, uncles, or cousins. It must be okay to buy for yourself. No one is buying for you. Nowhere is this factor more evident than in the evolution of China's Singles' Day holiday—which we introduced in Chapter 1 and which we will discuss in greater depth in Chapter 10—a kind of anti-Valentine's day that falls on November 11, into an explosion of consumerism.

4. **Collective experience; collective norms**: Juxtaposed against the impulse of individualism, there is also a strong Confucian ethos in China, that the individual has a responsibility to society and society prospers when everyone fits in. Individualism has limits. You are unlikely to see much in the way of a counterculture or flamboyantly out-of-sync behavior. Exhibitionism is frowned upon. Sociologist Erich Fromm noted that when people have the ability to be whatever they want, they want to be like everyone else. In China we see a similar 'herding effect' in which Internet trends have a special appeal, with its own slang term, 'wang hong', meaning an Internet trend or trendiness. By shopping you can assert your membership in a group as well as assert your personal identity. It is a tricky balance, but Chinese consumers pull it off.

We all like participating in group events, and we see this trend in Chinese popular culture. For example, the goal in karaoke is to do what everyone else is doing. The point of line dancing is to fit in. Popular culture is not to find yourself; it is to lose yourself. FOMO, the Fear of Missing Out, transcends cultures. But this trend is stronger in China than in the West because Confucian culture does not celebrate outliers as does the West. Social media reinforces this collective pattern so that shopping and dining are shared experiences. Opinions are crowd-sourced. And the merchants reinforce this pattern by supporting holiday sales, group buying, and other promotions. Consumers organize themselves for the expedition, and the brands organize as well.

Successful brands in China are able to tackle most or all of the above considerations. The consumer must not only be delighted with your product, they must also see a journey that respects these socio-cultural impulses.

5. **Health and safety**: Two of the more popular foreign market segments for Chinese consumers are nutrition and cosmetics. If you are putting a product in you or on you, you want to make sure it is safe. You do not mind paying a premium to ensure it has been inspected and tested by the appropriate foreign agencies. Japanese cosmetics and Australian agricultural products can both command a premium because of those countries' reputation for excellence in those respective market segments. Cosmetics is consistently the top-selling segment on Tmall; baby nutrition products and processed food products are all typically in the top five.

In sum, consumer behavior in China is driven in part by a series of social and cultural norms that transcend the functional utility of the product. There are emotional and psychological motivators of behavior which a successful brand should understand. People buy Fender guitars not just because they are an excellent product. Fenders also allow you to meet people and to share music. Fender stands not just for technical excellence. It stands for fun.

How to Win and Retain Loyal Customers in China

I was struck by a comment of a major luxury brand's CMO, who claimed that, 'the Chinese consumer isn't very loyal.' In my view, that is a misstatement or a misunderstanding of consumer behavior in China. The use of the word 'loyalty' in this sense is off-point for two reasons. First, because it could be perceived as condescending, or even insulting, implying that the consumer is under some sort of permanent obligation to stay with a brand. Second, it is exculpatory language, placing all responsibility on the consumer and none on the brand.

Rather than a brand stating that consumers are not loyal, a brand could equally well state that it is not very good at retaining customers.

Smart brands refresh themselves and engage in a permanent courtship. Less capable brands stagnate and complain that customers '. . . are not very loyal.'

It might be useful to understand the ways in which Chinese consumers differ from, say, western consumers. Foreign brands might perceive this as less loyalty, but I think there is something else at work. I have observed four persistent differences that define the China consumer market:

1   Weaker favorites
In many market segments, brand leadership is not well-established. In some segments, there is an absence of an incumbent or a legacy brand. This applies to many categories but seems more common in the premium and luxury space. Remember, prosperity is so recent to China that there are few consumers in the market who are repeat customers. Many Chinese are purchasing Nikes, for example, but a higher percentage will be purchasing them for the first time as compared to a western market. So, if you were responsible for marketing Beaujolais wines, it would not be a bad idea to partner with a bank's premium credit card department to offer affluent consumers a wine tasting and a short lecture on what makes a good wine.

2.   Demographic focus
The consumer population skews urban, young, affluent and female. They have the money and household influence, and smart brands are catering to this audience. For example, L'Oréal is addressing its audience in China by offering 'click-and-collect' experiences at duty-free retailers. Consumers can reserve products, pay for them online, and then pick them up at the airport. Smart brands also place a lot of focus on the millennial or post-millennial generation, and we will get to that in the section below.

3.   Digital footprint means digital pure play
In other words, brands can exist exclusively in ecommerce. There is no need to build out traditional bricks-and-mortar distribution. As mentioned at the start of this chapter, the Chinese consumer is digitally driven, both through discovery as well as through purchase. It's easy to be an absolutist here—if your brand is not communicating digitally, your brand is not communicating. That means engaging the consumer,

having a conversation with the consumer, even tantalizing the consumer. This digital reach is so strong that any brand can be a pure play digital brand.

Nike China understands this better than anyone, having recently introduced a mobile digital experience to give basketball fans an engaging view of what it's like competing in Nike's High School Basketball League (HBL), the ultimate high school sporting event in China.

On WeChat, Nike created 'The Road To HBL' that gives teens a first-hand look at what it's like to get into the team, looking at 'the training, the fun, the struggle, and glory of HBL.' Nike interviewed players, parents, friends, fans, and coaches and turned their stories into scenes.[*]

Nike has taken advantage of technology to shift corporate messaging. No longer is the brand talking to you, the brand is inviting you into its world and it empowers you to have the full brand experience.

4. A passion for novelty

The Chinese consumer has a passion for novelty. Consumerism is a journey. It is self-discovery. It is empowering to the individual.

For example, Mars overhauled its well-known Snickers bars by working with Alibaba to devise a spicy chili version just for China.[†] The bar resulted from research and surveys of Chinese consumers to discover that many craved spicy food and would be interested to try chocolate with a spicy kick. In the same vein, Listerine introduced a rosemary herb flavored version of their famous mouthwash.

Both projects relied on the 'Tmall Innovation Center' to survey consumers and respond to their demands by working with established brands, resulting in a highly successful new product.

All of this means a more experimental consumer mindset and arguably the most favorable opportunity for new brands in the world. The challenge, of course, is that it will take resources, creativity, and brand strength to capture this opportunity.

Are Chinese consumers loyal? Sure, if you fight for them.

---

[*] https://www.rga.com/work/case-studies/the-road-to-hbl
[†] https://www.alizila.com/alibaba-tmall-innovation-center-brands/

The March of the Post-Millennial Generation

I mentioned earlier that the consumer population skews toward youth and this point needs elaboration. Alibaba studied consumer behavior on its Tmall Global cross-border platform, and there is at least one clear finding every consumer brand in China should note: consumer spending is no longer driven by millennials, but by *post*-millennials.

By millennials, we mean consumers born between 1981 and 1996 (sometimes referred to as Gen Y). This is a key consumer demographic. As Benji Lamb, Director of China Business Development, Vitabiotics notes,

> . . . . there's a very strong millennial consumer base who are looking for new healthcare products, premium overseas healthcare products.[*]

Post-millennials—Gen Z—who were born between 1996 and 2010 and made up about 5 per cent of China's population,[†] spend an average of RMB25,000 (US $3600) a year on luxury goods, which is as much as their parents (the post- '65s or '70s generation).[‡] What's going on?

It should come as no surprise that the buzzy, youth-oriented brands lean toward Tmall Global, but the fact that 50 per cent of GMV (Gross Merchandise Value being the most widely used measure of sales as it comes before discounts and returns) comes from the post-millennial bracket is one of the strongest trends I have seen in China e-commerce.

Here's my take:

- Purchasing power booms in this age group. People are just starting in the workforce, and for many, this is the first time in their life they have an independent identity as a consumer. They can make purchases

---

[*] https://11-11.tswpp.com/vitamin-specialist-taps-into-health-demands-of-youngest-11-11-audience-ever/

[†] https://www.mckinsey.com/~/media/mckinsey/featured%20insights/china/china%20still%20the%20worlds%20growth%20engine%20after%20covid%2019/mckinsey%20china%20consumer%20report%202021.pdf

[‡] https://www.mckinsey.com/~/media/mckinsey/featured%20insights/china/how%20young%20chinese%20consumers%20are%20reshaping%20global%20luxury/mckinsey-china-luxury-report-2019-how-young-chinese-consumers-are-reshaping-global-luxury.ashx

without parental approval and they want to use this purchasing power to assert their identity. Consumerism is a display of self-expression. Not having kids adds to purchasing power.

- This is an experimental consumer culture. The South China Morning Post tells us:

Millennials push Chinese streetwear to new heights as they seek ways to express themselves . . . With money to spend and a willingness to take more risks than their global counterparts, China's post-'80s generation is blurring fashion's boundaries . . . *

This explains the weaker brand loyalty. If you are purchasing cosmetics for the first time, why not try alternative brands?

- A majority of the consumers are female. Males tend to take a more functional view toward appearance, meaning that clothes are merely a means to an end. Females are more likely to view appearance as part of their identity, meaning that apparel is part of the overall image and appeal. The most popular products in this segment are cosmetics, fragrance, and facial care products.
- Post-millennials are rising faster than millennials. Purchasing power more than doubles every decade in China. Fresh grads want to look good and maybe show off a bit. Remember: The high achievers in China are not in a bohemian culture or a counterculture.
- Just segmenting under-35 is not enough. There are big differences between millennials and post-millennials, with the latter more reliant on influencers, foreign culture, and experiences. They are on a quest.

The footloose nature of these consumers poses a special challenge for the brands. How do you reach the post-millennial?

- They are close to 100 per cent digital in how they process information, be it in music, movies, news or social connectivity.

---

* https://www.scmp.com/lifestyle/fashion-luxury/article/2103877/millennials-push-chinese-streetwear-new-heights-they-seek

- They have a penchant for novelty and generation-oriented products. Nobody wants your mom's cosmetics, except your mom. Every young person has a smartphone that can be used for augmented reality and virtual reality engagement.
- You need a social channel, not just a communications channel. You had better tell a story and not sell a product.
- The product is an enabler. Move beyond the pure function aspect of the product. How does it make you feel? What does it allow you to do? Every product is a lifestyle product.

Post-millennials are up for grabs. E-commerce is the best channel to grab them. Digital and social media outreach are the tools. Creativity is obligatory.

Cultural differences should facilitate, not impede, the transaction

Every society has cultural norms and preferences, and those in China might be among the strongest in the world. The strength of the culture does not mean that Chinese consumers are not open to foreign products. As I have noted before, Chinese consumers have a high capacity for experimentation and frequently become champions of foreign brands.

But the cultural dimension does have implications for marketing, both positive and negative. In a positive sense, you want to embrace local cultural norms and signifiers when you can. Chinese New Year promotions, anyone? In the Lego Chinese New Year construction set, the Lego figures carry with them *hongbao*—red packets—the obligatory gift of any visitor.

In a negative sense, you need to ensure there are not inadvertent cultural barriers that make your brand a challenge for the Chinese consumer. Make it as easy as possible for the consumer to fall in love with you.

The key point here is to develop a mechanism for screening your product, your brand, and your messaging so that you avoid the negative and promote the positive outcome.

You want to work with an advertising agency, a communications firm, your own team in China, or a specialized focus groups—probably with some sort of redundant combination—to test across the following areas:

Cultural Differences

- Diet. Our earlier peanut butter discussion reminds us that the Chinese diet has a range of differences. If you're selling anything that can be ingested, check your ingredients.

- Numbers and colors. Every society has their own superstitions surrounding luck and fortune. The number four isn't lucky because, in the Chinese language, 'four' is a homonym for 'death'. Six (lucky) and eight (lucky for money) are positive numbers. The color red is considered good, but you may want to stay away from green hats. Green hats were reserved as punishment for people who were related to prostitutes during the Yuan Dynasty. Even today, the phrase 'wearing a green hat' means that a wife has cheated on a husband.

- Names. You don't want the translation of your name to sound like it's something inauspicious. Sometimes a brand has a really savvy brand name in its home market, but when it goes to China it just doesn't translate or it's very hard for Chinese consumers to remember, say, or spell the name. You need to develop a Chinese name that works with the right characters and pronunciation.

- Regifting is popular, so make sure your packaging reflects the gift-giving holiday. Chinese consumers might give and regift as many mooncake packages as Americans might give and regift Christmas fruitcakes. Separately, it goes a long way if you give a little something extra—like a sample—with purchases for your brand. And those free samples can end up as a regift as well.

This is a reminder of a difference between Tmall and Amazon. You need to take steps on your Tmall store that might not be necessary for the US market, for the simple reason that Chinese consumers have faith in brands that actively engage with them and experiment, particularly if there is novelty or tech involved.

Key Takeaways

➤ Your three watchwords for marketing in China are: digital, social, and courtship.

➤ Beyond that, there are behavioral and societal norms you should play into and respect.

➤ Finally, there is the cultural dimension of your product, your brand name, and your messaging.

➤ You need to develop a mechanism to test for cultural or societal sensitivities.

8

Five Decisions Before You Start

Chinese consumers, especially younger generations, are becoming less price-sensitive by the day. Rather, price-to-perform is more important to them, and they tend to do a lot of research before buying. And with the emergence of shoppable live video, it means that they are eager to interact with brands and find out more about them and their products before buying. With the influx of brands and products entering the market each day, it is increasingly vital for brands to engage with consumers in fresh and memorable ways, and to show Chinese consumers that they are with them along their journeys, and that they care and respond to every bit of their concerns about the products.

—in conversation with Man-Chung Cheong, Insider Intelligence

Now that we have looked at the fundamentals of building good customer-brand relationships, this chapter examines key decisions each company must make before they launch in China.

Of course, a company can always adapt and change course. But it pays to conduct these exercises prior to launch and to regularly review them after you launch.

Every company that enters the China market has to grapple with five questions:

1. Do I use a distributor or an agent? A distributor purchases and then resells your goods. An agent handles your goods on your behalf but

does not take legal title. This difference has implications for profits, risk, and accounting.

2. Do I use a platform or a stand-alone site? A platform would be one of the multi-brand marketplaces such as Tmall or JD. A stand-alone site would be a site owned and managed by the brand.

3. Do I sell in-country or cross-border? You can take all of your product in-country so that the transaction occurs in China, or you can sell from off-shore so that the product enters China only after it is sold. This has implications for set-up costs, inventory management, delivery costs, and customs clearance.

4. How do I get ready for omnichannel, to make sure that my online and offline channels reinforce each other? As your online sales grow, you will be increasingly aware of off-line opportunities, and the off-line retailers will find you more attractive. What do you need to do in your early days to keep the door open for this possibility?

5. Are all my sales through proprietary channels or do I use third parties or informal channels such as daigous? China has an array of informal channels that can augment your official channels, but this also can mean giving up some control while gaining sales and exposure.

By the end of this chapter, after examining these essential questions, these important trade-offs, you should have gained a sense of the approach and have defined your goals.

Question One: Distributor or Agent?

Do I use a distributor or an agent? A distributor purchases and then resells your goods. An agent handles your goods on your behalf but does not take legal title. This difference has implications for profits, risk, and accounting.

Picture this: A global sports equipment company recently became frustrated by its sales in China. The company was experiencing strong growth from the tennis rackets it manufactures, but its badminton sales were a disappointment. Why the contrasting fortunes? Because the brand's Chinese distributor was refusing to stock the company's badminton equipment

'Don't blame me,' protested the distributor. 'Badminton isn't popular in China.' The distributor thought that if he stocked the inventory, it wouldn't sell to the pro shops across the country.

This is not how the relationship between manufacturers and distributors is supposed to work. In the traditional model, the distributor takes on the responsibility of marketing the products and growing the business. It's the distributor who establishes partnerships with wholesalers and retailers, keeping them supplied with the latest lines, stocking their inventory, and in return he can receive a margin upwards of 50 per cent.[*]

It's win-win, isn't it? Many brands simply don't have the resources to grow multiple specialized sales channels in-house, particularly in a large market like China. And if you are, for example, a processed food brand, it makes sense to work with a distributor that specializes in the food and beverage category because they will have working relations with major supermarket chains and wholesalers.

But what are the potential problems with this model in China?

First, the distributor can help you sell, but is less able to help you grow. The distributor has limited loyalty to the brand, particularly if its China sales numbers are modest or if it's a brand that is still relatively new to the market. Having a distributor provides a sales channel, but it does not provide a strategy. Many international brands are pleased with their distributor in their home market, but that's because they typically have far more control over the marketing activities and can communicate on local terms. They will often enjoy a stronger market position, a long-term relationship with the distributor, and home market advantages of advertising and word of mouth. It is easier for the relationship to be a win-win.

In China, however, these conditions rarely apply. The brand is often new to the market, doesn't yet command high revenue, and the distributor might be handling anywhere between 40 and 200 different brands. Some distributors might even be handling competitive brands unless you have

---

[*] Related themes are explored in Arnold, David, 'Seven Rules of International Distribution', *Harvard Business Review*, Nov.-Dec. 2000, https://hbr.org/2000/11/seven-rules-of-international-distribution

negotiated exclusivity. Why should they care about yours, particularly if other brands are growing faster?

So, if your brand is mid-size, say, a $300 million global brand and perhaps selling $10 million in China, how much work will a distributor do to help that $10 million grow to $15 million? In the same vein, you might have a new line of products that broaden the brand appeal by 10 per cent. Is the distributor going to stock these products for an extra $1 million in revenue? Not if there is an easier way to earn that $1 million. You might find yourself in a frustrating chicken-and-egg relationship. The distributor does not want to promote your product if it is not a winner, but the only way to make it a winner is to broaden its distribution.

E-commerce can be used to help in overcoming distribution problems like these, at least partially. An e-commerce channel allows you to build sales for your product, provides a basis for social media and advertising campaigns, and gives you proof of concept to help with distributors. E-commerce can also allow you to introduce new products and to experiment with seasonal bundles, key opinion leaders (KOLs), and other promotions. You are no longer subject to the preferences of the distributor.

An e-commerce approach also strengthens your ability to succeed in other channels. It means your supply chain is established, regulatory approval and labelling is complete, and your inventory is in the market. Now discussions with wholesalers and retailers take on a different hue. You have shown you are committed to the market.

Finally, e-commerce can also allow you to retain a better margin than working through a distributor. That distributor might charge a 50 per cent margin, but Tmall and JD both take single-digit commissions. There can be other fees, and advertising alone can easily be 20 per cent of your gross revenue. Even when all these costs are tallied up, a brand's bottom line in China can become more appealing through e-commerce than if it were totally reliant on a distributor.

Is your distributor your friend? Sure. Sort of. But the best approach in China might be to cultivate the distributor relationship for your high-volume items, and rely on e-commerce for the full product slate, new product launches, and customer engagement activities. Distributors are more likely to support you when they see that you have an e-commerce strategy. The best way of cultivating a friendship with that distributor is by first. cultivating a friendship with e-commerce. You are in charge of your own destiny. Go sell those badminton rackets.

Question Two: A Platform or a Stand-Alone Site?

Do I use a platform or a stand-alone site? A platform would be one of the multi-brand marketplaces such as Tmall or JD. A stand-alone site would be a site owned and managed by the brand.

This choice between a store on a platform or a stand-alone site, while seemingly simple, is complicated by the differences between Chinese and Western consumers when it comes to online shopping. In the United States and Europe, for example, shoppers tend to patronize stand-alone shopping websites that are owned and operated by familiar brands like Apple, Nike and Microsoft. In China, however, an online shopper is more likely to buy, say, an iPhone 12 from Apple's store on Tmall, than from Apple's own independent site in China. Some 97 per cent of China's consumer e-commerce is through a platform.[*]

This fact alone suggests a merchant's first choice when entering China ought to be a marketplace. That's where the traffic is. We will discuss platforms in Chapter 9, but it is worth noting that the Alibaba Group marketplaces, Taobao and Tmall, China's largest consumer-to-consumer (C2C) and business-to-consumer (B2C) websites respectively, together have more than 757 million annual active shoppers.[†] Their users are already in a buying mood and can be driven to a store organically through product search engines and promotions. The operators of stand-alone sites, on the other hand, must rely on their own resources to build traffic, starting from zero. Particularly if the brand is new-to-market or niche, this can be difficult and costly.

Marketplaces have two other advantages over stand-alone sites: trust and time.

---

[*] https://www.pwccn.com/en/retail-and-consumer/publications/total-retail-2017-china/total-retail-survey-2017-china-cut.pdf?utm_content=buffer28aaf&utm_medium=social&utm_source=twitter.com&utm_campaign=buffer#:~:text=Alibaba's%20Tmall%20platform%20dominates%20B2C,Tmall%20is%20just%20China's%20Amazon.

[†] https://www.alibabagroup.com/en/ir/presentations/pre201105.pdf

From a consumer trust standpoint, marketplaces have the edge. Tmall and JD, for example, authenticate the products they sell by only allowing brand owners or their authorized agents to operate stores on those platforms. Shoppers will have their payments held in escrow until they have received and are satisfied with the goods, thereby removing elements of the risk related to online shopping. 'Will my package arrive?' and 'Will the product match its description?' are questions that disappear when marketplaces act as honest brokers between merchants and buyers. Again, brands that are new to the China market have the most to gain by joining a marketplace, because they might otherwise struggle to win customers' trust.

Another element of trust helps the merchants. Unlike Amazon and other platforms, neither Alibaba nor JD develop their own products and brands to compete with those who sell on their platform. Merchants find it reassuring that they will not face competition from the very platform on which they are operating.

Time, too, is on the side of the marketplace. Web development and graphic design for a marketplace store is less demanding compared with building a stand-alone site from scratch, particularly one optimized for smartphones and tablets (which are essential in China). Marketplaces have dedicated teams that build seamless, user-friendly mobile apps; they also have battle-tested networks and can provide technical support and marketing guidance, allowing merchants to more selectively dedicate resources and minimize overhead.

Yet we are not about to close the door on stand-alone sites, which have advantages in the areas of control, transaction costs and flexibility. With a stand-alone site, the merchant maintains complete control over service policies, web design, and customer data. Merchants can set the pace for how to deal with returns, customer inquiries, and product reviews, and can tailor store design and navigation to suit precisely the desired brand image.

Merchants may also experience lower transaction costs as they are not required to pay 2–5 per cent of sales to the marketplace operator. In comparison, these platform fees are a bargain. In the United States, Amazon charges 15 per cent of gross sales in categories such as beauty, footwear, and personal care.

Finally, stand-alone sites offer flexibility in introducing new products and managing inventory. In marketplaces, new product listings require approval from the operator, which can take weeks or even months. When you run your own site, you can introduce new products at your own pace. Marketplaces tend to have strict inventory requirements which forbid the merchant from selling if the goods are not in stock. However, on stand-alone sites a merchant with some empty bins has the option of continuing to take orders and notifying consumers that shipping will be delayed.

Considering all these factors, the marketplace versus stand-alone decision ultimately hinges on a company's size, strategy, and resources. Generally speaking, merchants wanting speed-to-market and low costs should gravitate to marketplaces, while deeper-pocketed brands with online experience and existing e-commerce assets might find the stand-alone route relatively appealing.

But here's the key: these solutions are not mutually exclusive. We normally recommend a two-pronged approach. First, use a platform store to get in front of as many consumers as possible and to capture transactions. Second, use a stand-alone site for brand awareness and education. World-class brands such as Mars and 3M use this approach. Their stand-alone sites focus on brand stories, product origins, and news releases, while the bulk of sales activity takes place on platforms. Using the right approach for each channel gives brands the opportunity to connect with a broad range of potential customers.

Question Three: In-Country or Cross-Border Solution?

Do I sell in-country or cross-border? You can take all of your product in-country so that the transaction occurs in China, or you can sell from off-shore so that the product enters China only after it is sold. This has implications for set-up costs, inventory management, delivery costs, and customs clearance.

During a periodic strategic review with an international sales leader from a fast-growing US cosmetics brand I had the chance to discuss their China strategy. This brand had seen—and won, actually—rapid success through cross-border e-commerce in China and was now trying to think through its in-country strategy. It had done the legal work to protect its trademark in China but had to work through the cost/benefit and timing of setting up an in-country e-commerce store. What was my advice?

First, an overview of cross-border and in-country. By cross-border, I mean channels such as Tmall Global or JD Worldwide which allow foreign brands to sell to Chinese consumers from outside of mainland China, be it from the United States, Hong Kong, or a specially designated Free Trade Zone. With cross-border e-commerce, Chinese consumers are able to experience the brand in a local format (the digital experience is the same as in-country) but buy from abroad. And the product is held offshore until sold.

In-country solutions tend to be favored by the larger and more-established brands because the greater the volume of sales, the more business sense it makes to import the product and build out local logistics and distribution. Smaller and new-to-market brands tend to use a cross-border solution to test the market without the up-front costs of inventory and regulatory approval.

Cross-border model

There are several advantages to the cross-border model: The brand faces lower Chinese regulatory, testing, and approval hurdles. There are some market segments where this becomes crucial, such as cosmetic brands that do not allow animal testing. Additionally, the time-to-launch can be a few months shorter than in-country. VAT/tariffs are applied post-sales, as opposed to pre-sales with in-country. New-to-market brands often undertake market discovery through cross-border to gain an understanding of consumer preference as it relates to SKUs, pricing, and communication—without having to invest heavily in inventory, offline marketing and primary research. Finally, there are some *de minimis* exemptions for duties and customs that apply to the cross-border model.

But there are downsides to the cross-border model as well. Unit logistics costs, which in one form or another are passed to the customer, tend to be higher since products enter China one order at a time. Also, shipping fees are a bit higher than with the in-country model, since China Customs has to process each individual order as it enters the market. Cross-border also involves a prohibitive returns process, and this means less customer connectivity. Finally, there is a cap on the *de minimis* tax exemptions. The limit on a single transaction is about US$730 and the annual limit for individual consumers on cross-border e-commerce is just under US$3800.*

In-country model

The in-country model involves higher start-up costs, including compliance and inventory. But in some cases, it offers lower overall prices to consumers. And there are three overriding benefits to the in-country model. First, your shipping times are shorter—same-day or one-day for all tier-one cities, versus two to four days from a Free Trade Zone. Second, you are able to offer customers the option to return the product, no questions asked. Third, the numbers are simply greater. There are more consumers who think and act in domestic terms than there are those who tend to purchase internationally. So, if your aspiration is to go to a wider audience, the domestic variant of Tmall, JD, and PDD is your ticket.

Which one is best?

So, what was my advice to the cosmetics brand? (1) They had already proven their success on the cross-border platform and were ready to move in-country. (2) Start with a limited number of SKUs on the in-country platform, adding as volume grows. (3) Keep the cross-border store open for at least 6–12 months because consumers will be more familiar with it and it will be able to support a broader array of SKUs. (4) Approach Singles' Day (November 11)—which we have already briefly discussed and will delve into further in Chapter 10—as not just the most important B2C day of the year, but also as the most important B2B day of the year. Every retail chain in China will be looking at the major platforms to see what promising brands can be successful off-line, and 11.11 should be treated as the proving ground for demand and if you're selling in-country, by definition you are compliant for offline retail.

---

* https://www.china-briefing.com/news/chinas-crackdown-daigou-cross-border-e-commerce-policies/

This particular advice might not fit every brand, but the logic behind the advice is broadly applicable. Success in China requires a bit of persistence, a bit of flexibility, a bit of creativity, and, as we see in the in-country/cross-border discussion, the ability to calibrate effort to opportunity. Expanding resources as the situation warrants and always leaning a bit forward in the market are best practices that should be applied to international expansion in general; they are ever more pertinent to China, where complexities run nearly as high as the sales opportunity.

Question Four: Getting Ready for Omnichannel

How do I get ready for omnichannel? As your online sales grow, you will be increasingly aware of off-line opportunities, and the traditional off-line retailers will find you more attractive. What do you need to do in your early days to keep the door open for this possibility?

Brands want to make sure their sales channels reinforce each other, provide for a better customer experience, and respect the trend of consumers migrating to e-commerce without undermining a profitable store-based business.

The emphasis international brands place on China e-commerce is not a surprise given the size of the market and the rapid rates of growth. But what are the omnichannel guidelines to drive sales and increase engagement and retention? There are a few rules to keep in mind:

Love all your channels

The moment a customer encounters your brand is the moment he or she starts to determine its value. Therefore, the first step in using omnichannel effectively is to maximize performance within each channel. A low-growth channel might have high absolute numbers. A transaction through one channel might be the result of unknown interactions through another channel. So, it's essential to bring a strong brand image and well-trained customer service team to each channel. Love all your channels because those channels allow your customer to love your brand.

Look at Starbucks: It complements its 4400 store* locations in China with coupons, mobile payment options, and loyalty programs available on the Starbucks app as well as its WeChat account and its Tmall store. Customers not only encounter knowledgeable staff at the stores, but can also reach out to the brand digitally, receiving a response within seconds. Starbucks knows that although the transactions take place in stores, brand identity and consumer engagement is overwhelmingly digital.

Stay consistent: Do no harm

Maintain consistent communications, pricing, and customer service across channels. The online and offline experience has to offer the same brand image and transaction possibilities. Same identity, message, and pricing. Pricing consistency will avoid internal and external conflict, as your store managers and e-commerce teams won't be competing against each other and customers won't feel like they missed out by not shopping on a specific channel.

Similarly, train customer service teams on each aspect of product introductions and promotions using standardized material. In addition, give your online merchandising and graphic design the same look and feel of your physical store.

While I was reading a magazine on a business trip to London, out falls a 'blow-in' card for Charles Tyrwhitt, a prominent shirt-maker, good for £10 off any purchase, online or offline. I can bring the card into any store, or I can use the card online because it has a serial number that I can key in. Lovely. Tyrwhitt understands the consistency principle—and a whole lot more, we assume.

The easy cross-sell: Cross-promotion

It is not enough merely to be consistent. You must also use your channels to cross-sell. Make sure that each channel promotes and validates the other. All printed and in-store material should act as a gateway to the

---

* https://www.starbucks.com.cn/en/about/

brand's digital realm; think QR code or hashtag. All online purchases should insert material with store locations with the shipments. The online store should offer a locator map for offline stores. Check your receipt next time you shop. If a URL or QR code is printed at the bottom, this brand understands cross-promotion.

The harder cross-sell: One window to the customer

Regardless of what the customer is doing with the merchant, regardless of where, and regardless of what channel—the store has one aggregate view of the customer and the customer has one aggregate view of the store. So, the customer can purchase online and return at a store. The customer can visit a store and then order online. Harder to do than it sounds. And harder still across multiple markets. Yet I can use my Citibank ATM card in Shanghai, Washington DC, or Singapore and they immediately identify me. What kind of loyalty program does your store have and how does it function across borders?

The trend is your friend

Let's not pretend that O2O is a static situation and we are discussing coordination among equal channels. Indeed, perhaps the strongest trend in retail today is the move away from stores to e-commerce. We see this in every market in the world and across every demographic. Some areas— like China—are moving faster than others, but everybody is moving. No surprise here. Consumers have better selection and better discovery mechanisms. On-line merchants have lower costs and can more easily experiment. But how do you play into this trend?

The most important lesson here for merchants and brand owners is that you will be better off if you run your e-commerce program directly. As we discussed in an earlier post, do not leave this to your distributor. Your net performance will improve. You will retain control of your brand. And you will drive offline improvement through online improvement. Bring in outside expertise as needed. But the smarter brands will seek to run their China e-commerce operations aggressively, purposefully and directly.

Question Five: Daigous and Third Parties, More Friends

Are my sales all through proprietary channels or do I use daigous and third-parties? China has an array of informal channels that can augment your official channels, but this also can mean giving up some control while gaining sales and exposure.

During a lunch meeting in Los Angeles, a friend showed up with some products he had just purchased from the local CVS drugstore. When he relayed that the purchases were to be shipped to relatives in China, I observed that the products were already available there. He agreed, but said that his in-laws preferred products shipped directly from the United States.

'So, you are a one-man daigou,' I commented, and he nodded in agreement.

Daigous are one of the least understood sales channels in China, in some cases successful because there is no 'official' branded e-commerce store. But even when daigou stores and official stores co-exist, the daigou channel can make up an important component of sales. What is a daigou and how can a brand use this channel to drive sales?

Daigou (pronounced dye-go) literally means 'representative purchasing' and refers to merchants who source and re-sell products even if they are not authorized distributors. It is essentially an informal consumer-to-consumer channel. They proliferate in the Chinese e-commerce ecosystem, with several advantages for the Chinese consumer:

- **First, these personal shoppers provide a customized shopping experience**: Chinese consumers engage the daigou with a problem or a need. The daigou helps educate the consumer and provides a solution. Daigou agents tend to live outside of China and can obtain quality foreign products. Thus, the daigou is typically demand-driven, with little in-stock inventory—although this is changing.
- **Second, daigous provide authenticity**: Daigou products are sourced directly from the country of origin. Some Chinese consumers, such as the in-laws mentioned earlier, believe the products sold in China are different from those sold in their home market. Others might fear adulteration or do not trust the supply chain. Daigous address those

concerns and a typical daigou web page will show where the product was sourced, even displaying a photo of the purchaser and her family buying the product or livestreaming the purchase from the store while she selects and purchases products.

- **Third, daigous can offer better deals or better selection than the official stores**: Official outlets might raise the China selling price due to tariffs or additional marketing and operational costs. Daigous are often individuals or small companies who can live with a lower margin. The result is lower prices for Chinese consumers.

In the early days of China e-commerce, a typical daigou was a student or a tourist who could bring back a duffle bag of products to sell online. This has now evolved to where the daigous are much larger, more business-like, and can have formal relations with brands. Frontier Strategy Group estimates that 7 per cent of China e-commerce takes place through daigou channels.[*] For their part, brands are increasingly likely to actively manage the daigou.

The categories with the most daigou activity: Luxury apparel and accessories, cosmetics—especially those that are cruelty-free—and nutrition, including mother and baby products. Taobao has long been the primary platform for daigou merchants, although WeChat is gradually becoming more active. And daigous are not just for the US market; Australia and New Zealand have huge daigou ecosystems as do many European countries.

Chinese Government View

The Chinese government has been largely supportive of the daigous, realizing that they fill a market need by helping when a brand will not enter the China market or will not effectively connect with the Chinese consumer. At the same time, there is a concern about daigous who might be taking advantage of loopholes.

---

[*] https://blog.frontierstrategygroup.com/2018/08/daigou-what-you-need-to-know-about-chinas-newest-e-commerce-opportunity/

These concerns center on tax evasion and on product safety and dependability, so China customs will often check matters such as expiration dates and product authenticity. And there are a few other changes. Daigou agents are now required by Chinese law to register.* This means their business must be connected to a Chinese entity and taxes must be paid on products brought across the border. No more students with duffle bags.

For their part, WeChat and Taobao have taken steps to identify unregistered daigou agents on their platforms and remove their posts and listings. Daigous can be a helpful addition to your marketing strategy but make sure you work only with legally registered and professional entities.

Beyond daigous, you will find an array of independent stores, multi-brand stores, and other outlets that can help build sales. If you manufacture specialty food products, for example, you will find stores that specialize in organic products, or a special cuisine that could well stock your goods. Or you can sell your sun cream through a store that sells swimwear. The point is that your e-commerce flagship store will build credibility and allow you to start your outreach to these important third parties.

Three Daigou Lessons

These trends indicate that even as daigous sales grow, they will be fewer but more professional. How should this affect brand behavior?

First, the daigou market has been a central driver of Chinese consumers' internationalization and brand education. Professional daigou agents have a book of loyal customers who trust them not only to provide a quality product, but to recommend new products the agent deems suitable for their customers' lifestyles. Much ado is made about the emphasis placed on solid relationships in Chinese culture, and that dynamic is on full display in the daigou market.

Second, serious daigou agents are not scared by the new policies, and indeed embrace them. Legitimate daigous have the resources to build their businesses and fully comply with local laws. Although there may be adjustments to their economics, these daigous welcome the extra scrutiny

---

* https://www.china-briefing.com/news/chinas-crackdown-daigou-cross-border-e-commerce-policies/

as it weeds out bad actors. This 'flight to quality' means an increase in consumer spending through this channel, with a skew toward the stronger daigous.

Most importantly: The daigou is your friend. Brands should not view daigou agents as competition for official channels—on the contrary. Daigou agents are some of the strongest brand advocates and are actively helping brands acquire and retain customers. Savvy brands embrace daigous as partners and find ways to help their businesses grow. In this new commercial environment, brands that use daigous as force multipliers have the most to gain.

Key Takeaways

A successful China initiative will involve a series of high-level tactical decisions such as distributor or agent; platform or stand-alone; in-country or cross-border; omnichannel; and daigous.

➢ These questions involve trade-offs, but most decisions can be adjusted or augmented as you go along.

➢ Calibrate the complexity of your decisions to your sales volume. The management bandwidth you apply to China should be commensurate with the value of the market.

➢ For mid-tier and junior brands this likely means you start with a single store on a major platform, and you start with a cross-border model. You must be prepared to run your store with an agent as distributors will not be easy to find for a new-to-market brand.

9

Platforms and Social Media

China is the rapidly advancing frontier of ecommerce. It is bigger and simply better than everywhere else. Alibaba is now 5+ years ahead of Amazon in sophistication—and pulling away.

—in conversation with Jeff Towson, Professor, Beijing University

In Chapter 8 we discussed the importance of using an e-commerce platform in China rather than a stand-alone site. In this chapter, we will take you into China's e-commerce ecosystem and introduce you to the leading platforms. Additionally, we will showcase the leading social commerce and social media outlets.

The Three Top E-Commerce Players

Let's first take a look at the three big players whose platforms have wowed consumers throughout China and increasingly around the world. When we look at the share of sales of the top marketplaces, we see a sharp concentration. Alibaba has 50.1 per cent of retail e-commerce in China, JD has 26.5 per cent and Pinduoduo has 12.8 per cent.[*] [and †]

---

[*] https://www.webretailer.com/b/online-marketplaces-china/

[†] https://www.statista.com/statistics/880212/sales-share-of-the-leading-e-commerce-retailers-in-china/

	Alibaba	JD	Pinduoduo
Visits per Month (million)	Tmall: 177 Taobao: 455	285	288
Active customers (million)	726	417	628
Retail GMV ($billion)	$969	$513	$248
Most popular market segments	Cosmetics and apparel	Consumer electronics and smartphones	Household Essentials (toilet paper and lightbulbs)

Why we like Alibaba

The three most important Alibaba platforms for foreign businesses are Tmall, its cross-border variant Tmall Global, and Taobao.

Tmall / Tmall Global—This joint platform is the leading B2C site in China, actually the leading B2C site in the world. I call it a joint platform because even though there are separate approaches for the merchant, the two channels are combined for the Chinese consumer, who will see them both through the same web site. However, each store on the web site will be designated either Tmall or Tmall Global.

TaoBao—An online C2C shopping platform. Whereas Tmall and Tmall Global only allow authorized stores to operate, TaoBao allows anyone to sell anything, in this sense similar to eBay.

Still, why should you focus on Tmall first? In short, Tmall commands a priority because it is massive and because it is really, really good.

But there is something beyond the sheer functionality and utility of Tmall. Tmall provides a personally customized store experience for the consumer, links the consumer to off-line outlets, and provides new opportunities for brand narratives, livestreaming and other forms of content distribution.

As your brand builds out its Tmall presence, bear in mind the core tools on the Alibaba platform. A successful store needs to actively manage a creative, forward-leaning marketing strategy with multiple consumer touch-points and the capacity for controlled experimentation.

Here are five approaches to help your Tmall growth stay on track:

First, an engagement strategy: A successful Tmall store requires customized communications and personalized messaging. The merchant needs to continue to court the consumer. You are not just displaying goods, but you are having a conversation with the customer. A home page should adapt to the customer's gender and purchasing history. You need a loyalty program and a high-touch customer relationship management system.

Second, content marketing: Weitao is Alibaba's built-in social feed for Tmall and Taobao. It lets KOLs and brands post product and lifestyle content, build an audience, and engage with potential buyers. Consumers use Weitao to research brands and products through an entertaining format. Keep your store's Weitao content current and updated as Alibaba uses AI and its users' digital behavior to push traffic to—or from—various Weitao streams.

Another aspect of content marketing is Taobao Livestream, an in-platform mechanism through which stores can engage KOLs to introduce their products to new customers. This is discussed more deeply in Chapter 12, but frequent livestreaming is a powerful tool in targeting broader audiences and driving sales momentum during promotions. It allows you to display your product in an active, real-world setting.

Third, group buy: Juhuasuan (JHS) is Alibaba's group-buying platform. Although part of the Alibaba family, JHS has a separate platform, with shoppers seamlessly linked to it through Tmall and Taobao. JHS is particularly important for new-to-market brands that need to acquire first-time customers because it allows buyers to try a new product at a discounted price. JHS offers both single-product and grouped promotions, each lasting for up to three days, with a preview period beforehand to warm up the customer base.

To participate in a JHS single-product promotion, you need to have the specified inventory on hand, such as a minimum of RMB 1 million worth of goods. Second, you also need to have an established track record of sales. Third, you need to be willing to offer a discount on your product, typically at least 20 per cent.

In JHS grouped promotions, five to ten brands that meet the above criteria are linked together in a single event, with each brand offering two or three products. The brands will be in a common category such as beauty or nutrition, with a landing page constructed for the event. As all participating brands will run marketing for the grouped promotion, each brand receives a boost from the collective marketing effort.

Fourth, Taobao Headlines (or 'Star Shop'): This is an Alibaba advertising unit exclusively for flagship stores, also personalized to the customer. It's a display ad delivered to the top of search results that pushes traffic directly to flagship stores, at a fee per thousand impressions. With Alibaba's programmatic advertising technology, merchants can customize banner content based on target audiences.

Fifth, in-platform promotion tools: Tmall has 'recommended' or 'must buy' product listings that encourage users to add items to their shopping carts. Similarly, Tmall has a 'good products' process that utilizes users' browsing preferences to feed them personalized content. In addition, Alibaba has tools for lead generation and sales through rebates. There are also additional affiliate marketing programs in which your store gives other stores a commission for sales they generate on your behalf.

In sum, Tmall is a dynamic platform with a wide array of marketing tools that provide significant opportunities for customization and traffic generation. But brands need to have an appetite for experimentation and the ability to put some resources into the store to take full advantage of what Tmall has to offer. Tmall has the potential to take Chinese consumers on the best e-commerce journey in the world. Make sure your brand can greet these consumers along the way.

Why we like JD

While the majority of companies will first pursue a Tmall strategy, international brands in China may want to pursue a JD strategy, too.

The core difference between China's two leading e-commerce companies: Alibaba runs Tmall, the largest e-commerce platform in the world. For the most part, Alibaba does not purchase products. JD, on the other hand, runs its e-commerce operations more as a traditional online retailer like Walmart—not surprising as Walmart owns some 12 per cent of JD—in which it purchases and resells. Again, like Walmart, it has built its model on high-volume and low margins to deliver considerable value to Chinese consumers.

Similar to Alibaba, JD offers both in-country and cross-border channels, JD.com and JD Worldwide. The merchant has to decide which channel to use but the consumer sees them both on the same platform.

Each of these giants will also compete in the other's lane. Tmall will purchase and resell some products, notably groceries, and JD also runs an online platform. And JD offers many of the same benefits as Tmall such as livestream, daily promotions, and personalized recommendations.*

Here are four key attributes of JD:

Authentic goods only: JD billboards their 'zero tolerance' policy for counterfeit products. This is a strong opening statement and a key part of their positioning strategy.

Logistics and partnerships: JD is able to offer a high-touch, high-quality logistics service including superior delivery times. This in-house system covers 99 per cent of China's population, an impressive feat in itself. This success is due to their extensive warehouse and distribution network, self-owned and -operated logistics fleet. Remember, JD introduced same-day delivery. If you order by 11 a.m., your product will be delivered the same day. Also worth noting in logistics, JD offers free delivery to Hong Kong, Macau, and Taiwan—a sure sign that JD is spreading its wings beyond the mainland.

Last-mile delivery: JD uses its own uniformed staff to handle the last mile, delivered with speed, quality, and a smile. And they are testing unmanned delivery vehicles such as cars, carts and drones. JD also has a number of

---

* http://www.woshipm.com/pd/684862.html

initiatives underway using AI and AR/VR technology to ensure consumer trust and enhance the consumer experience. For example, JD offers an AR-enabled app called JD Dream to allow shoppers to step into a virtual reality shopping experience to browse and buy products on JD.com, or to preview how a piece of furniture would look in their own homes.

The result: In 2020, JD reported Singles' Day sales of US$41 billion— compared to Alibaba's US$74 billion.* While coming in second, US$41 billion is a huge figure; in fact, Amazon had only $10.4 billion on Prime Day in the United States in 2020. More importantly, it serves as a reminder that international brands need to develop a JD strategy as they approach the China market.

Why We Like Pinduoduo

Pinduoduo is like Groupon with games and social networking mixed in. The platform allows users to invite their friends and family to join in purchasing the same product in order to get discounts utilizing a group-buying model. There is even a dashboard to keep track of which users saved the most by inviting friends to purchase with them. The platform combines a group-buying model with inexpensive products and social media. In addition, gaming-type promotions such as one-hour specials, cash rewards for daily check-ins, price cuts, lotteries, and lucky draws are blended in to encourage impulse shopping and make it entertaining and fun.

Pinduoduo's distinction is 'social e-commerce' and it does well with the bargain-oriented and social-oriented consumer. Its stronger market segments are household basics, food, and affordable items.

A large part of PDD's growth has been driven by the fact that it can be accessed through the WeChat messaging service, which has over a billion monthly users. WeChat is a key part of daily life in China and allows people to make payments within the app.

---

* https://www.cnbc.com/2020/11/12/singles-day-2020-alibaba-and-jd-rack-up-record-115-billion-of-sales.html

PDD has stickier, but less affluent customers. PDD customers are more likely to return to the site, but the average per capita spend on the platform was RMB 1993. By comparison, annual spend per active buyer on Alibaba was around RMB 9000 per buyer, and approximately RMB 6000 on JD.com.*

Because of this more mass-market appeal, PDD is not a natural starting point for international brands, and PDD's team seems to have less experience in dealing with international companies.

Does the rise of PDD mean that Chinese online consumer preferences are moving down market? Call it a consumption downgrade if you prefer, but after years of high growth in the luxury and premium segments there is some evidence that the fastest-growing online segment today is the mass market.

There are two trends at work: the evolution of Chinese consumers and the maturity of Chinese brands.

First, the evolution of Chinese consumers: The profile of online Chinese consumers has evolved over the past few years because of the ongoing tech empowerment of the middle class and lower middle class. In other words, the early tech adopters in any society tend to be the more educated and the more affluent. These demographics formed the bulk of e-commerce shoppers over the past decade and are still the most significant shopping group in China.

But over time, the less affluent and more remote consumers are learning to love e-commerce as well. They increasingly have smart phones and internet connectivity, and they are becoming more comfortable with online lifestyle and purchases, an area originally the home territory for the young and wealthy.

The rapid access of Pinduoduo reflects this trend of the emerging tech middle class. So, we are seeing a run-up in sales of instant noodles, paper towels, and value-oriented consumer products.

It is not that the market is moving down, but that a new middle class is more active. The luxury and premium segments continue to grow nicely in China, but the mass-market segment is growing faster.

---

* https://technode.com/2020/11/13/pinduoduo-shares-soar-20-on-q3-earnings-surprise/

Second, the maturity of Chinese brands: The country's manufacturers, retailers, and brand managers are increasingly sophisticated, from merchandising to product design to quality control. They know they cannot go head-to-head with, say, Louis Vuitton, but home-grown heroes such as Xiaomi and Huawei will gladly go up against the likes of Apple and Samsung. The mass market is increasingly dominated by local brands. Marketing guru Tom Doctoroff noted,

> Two years ago, 32 of the top 50 brands [in China] were multinational brands. Today, 30 are from the mainland.*

It is just that there are more Chinese consumers than ever before and more Chinese brands than ever before. What should international brands do in this evolving landscape?

1. **Maintain brand integrity**: Do not devalue your brand by chasing market segments traditionally not part of your target market. Smart brands know this, which is why you will not find a down-market version of Nike or Levi's or Starbucks or Apple. These great brands might offer unadorned versions of their products for the starter consumer, but they are not chasing the mass market.

2. **Don't freeze**: It is a mistake to chase the market if that means forsaking your brand identity. And the lower you go the more you are competing on price. But that having been said, think about how to experiment in the middle market or how to start a conversation with these new consumers. More pop-up stores? More entry-point pricing? More instructional videos? Don't be so indifferent to the middle market that you do not have the capacity to experiment.

3. **Refresh your brand**: As mass market brands grow in acceptance, it behoves the premium brands to create new expectations, demonstrate their value in distinctive ways, and focus on additional benefits for consumers. Some people choose to fly economy class and some choose

---

* https://www.nanjingmarketinggroup.com/blog/innate-advantages-western-brands-have-in-china-part-2

business class. For your business, make sure that the business class experience delivers exceptional value to the consumer.

4. **Remember the network**: Chinese consumers think digitally and so should you. Your brand story should be as much network-oriented as product-oriented. What celebrities are using your product? Does your loyalty program have meetups in NYC and Shanghai? How can you make your consumer base a fan club? Smart brands actively communicate with their customers to build brand passion. Remember, the appeal of the product goes beyond the product itself to what the product enables the consumer to do.

Social Commerce

Beyond the big three e-commerce platforms, there are also powerful social commerce platforms. By 'Social Commerce' I mean platforms that originally began as social outlets and in the past few years have added e-commerce sales channels. Their e-commerce sales are smaller than the Big Three, but they have powerful reach because of their social strength.

WeChat—1.2 billion Monthly Active Users (MAU):[*] WeChat is used for messaging, social media, playing games, and making purchases. WeChat is as much a platform as a service, composed of interest groups and mini-apps, small programs and games that are created by businesses, and easy to download. Everyday there are 45 billion messages sent on WeChat.[†] In 2019, the number of mini-apps through WeChat reached 2.36 million, with a user base of more than 840 million[‡] and WeChat mini-apps emerged with more than 800 billion RMB of transactions.[§]

---

[*] Kawo—the ultimate introduction to social media in China.

[†] Ibid.

[‡] https://www.melchers.com.hk/wechat-mini-programs-a-rapidly-growing-trading-channel-in-china/#:~:text=At%20the%202020%20WeChat%20Open,45%25%20from%20the%20year%20before.&text=Younger%20users%20predominate%20on%20WeChat,aged%20between%2018%20and%2040.

[§] https://walkthechat.com/%c2%a5800-billion-wechat-mini-program-transaction-volume-in-2019-tencent-annual-report/

Little Red Book (or Xiaohongshu)—100 Million MAU: Popular with women, Little Red Book started off as a Yelp-like review site and now has broadened, allowing users to not only comment but also make purchases. Little Red Book allows influencers and users to leave comments, drive traffic with paid posts, and improve brand awareness and search any trending relevance. With a user profile that skews female, 67 per cent of products sold were skincare and make-up, with brands from the US, Japan and France topping the sales.[*] Louis Vuitton became the first luxury brand to livestream on Xiaohongshu, resulting in over 15,000 viewers.[†]

Social Media, entertainment, and search

Social media permeates all aspects of life in China, including news, entertainment, communication, eating, dating, education, health, and work and professional activity.

Douyin (internationally known as TikTok)—513 million MAU: In America, it may still be known as a dance video app. But in China, Douyin reaches consumers with content such as a hyper-speed step-by-step makeup look, or a brand ambassador with a product placement, or a company introducing its brand history. These videos are like shortened commercials, and show something fun and unique, whether it's a product tutorial, a product launch, or a holiday promotion. The platform makes video editing easy and comes with a fun array of effects.

Weibo—550 million MAU: Weibo is a multi-faceted content-sharing social media site, like Twitter. It's an open platform, free to post, and can help with brand awareness.

Baidu: China's largest search engine. Baidu accounts for 80 per cent of the market share in China and handles an average of 6 billion search queries

---

[*] https://www.sohu.com/a/437633113_100211024
[†] https://daxueconsulting.com/louis-vuitton-in-china/

per day in China alone.* By comparison, Google sees some 12 billion searches in the US each month.†

Four keys to China's digital ecosystem

Going through a list of social media platforms and their attributes can be a bit confusing. As impressive as the numbers are, it is difficult for non-users to keep the various platforms straight or to fully understand the differences.

This takes us to the first key: there is a trade-off between comprehensive coverage and simplicity. If you are new to market and mid-size, I would normally recommend starting with one sales platform and two to three social media platforms.

The second key is that the digital landscape in China is still evolving. Douyin is only six years old and is now the largest short-form video platform in the world. Over time, you are going to want to experiment with different channels and approaches.

The third key: It is a mini-app world. Alibaba, WeChat, Baidu and Douyin all offer a cluster of hundreds of apps, called mini-apps within their platform to facilitate everything from instant messaging to payments. Increasingly, corporations and brands develop their own mini-apps to be used on the major platforms. We will discuss mini-apps more in Chapter 12.

The final key to understanding: Every player is changing lanes. WeChat and Douyin have moved into e-commerce. Alibaba has Youku, a video service and Weitao, a social media platform. Baidu has a video channel, iQiYi, similar to Netflix. This means that brands will have to continually experiment with new channels in order to keep pace.

Why do consumers like Platforms?

The broader question is: Why do platforms work? My theory: because they fit with consumer psychology in an era of mass prosperity.

---

* https://www.brightedge.com/resources/whitepapers/seo-and-paid-success-internationally
† https://www.statista.com/statistics/265796/us-search-engines-ranked-by-number-of-core-searches/#:~:text=In%20July%202020%2C%20Verizon%20Media,the%20U.S.%20desktop%20search%20queries.

Before societies attained general prosperity, consumer spending focused overwhelmingly on necessities and behavior was linear. People need certain items and they purchase them. In prosperous societies, consumer spending focuses on discretionary purchases and consumer behavior is non-linear. The journey involves at least five key steps:

Discovery: What's out there? Why should I fall in love with it? Yesterday's consumers went to the store with a shopping list, knowing what they needed. Today's consumers go to the store in the hopes of being convinced they need something. They view shopping online as a discovery process. I might need something. Court me. Enchant me. Seduce me.

Engagement: Can the brand have a conversation with the consumer? Why should the consumer listen to the brand? Does the brand have the capacity to listen as well?

Entertainment: Dazzle me. Make me laugh. Tell me something useful. Use video. Let me play a game.

Validation: Do my friends approve? What about KOLs? I want to feel good about this purchase.

Transaction mechanics: Make it fast and simple, with consumer protection.

So, a consumer today might know she needs a tennis racket but has only a vague opinion of what brand and style. She won't find a better selection and better range of prices than on Tmall. Beyond that, the consumer can easily check online for data points such as which brand of rackets was used by the winners at the French Open and her decision is guided. The platform to the rescue.

Or, what if a consumer has to purchase something for her boyfriend—a more challenging consumer journey to be sure—and she is at a loss as to what to buy. She can search online for generic answers such as 'Most popular birthday gifts for men' or 'Most popular men's apparel items'. Relationship saved.

Every consumer has a different appetite for these five steps and every brand has a different commitment or competency in undertaking them. Hence the enormous value of Tmall. One brand might fall short, but the platform in general will come through.

So Tmall is not just about consumer choice. It is about consumer psychology.

Increasingly, the consumer journey is as important as the destination. And, from our standpoint, Tmall offers the best journey around.

The bottom line: China is changing and the competitive map is changing with it. You are not going to reach next year's target numbers with last year's strategy. Your brand has to manage the complexity and rapid changes of China's digital ecosystem and this means a willingness to invest in the market and an ongoing capacity for experimentation.

Key Takeaways

➤ Hunt with the pack. Start with the major platforms and channels. You need eyeballs.
➤ Add complexity as you add revenue.
➤ With an evolving e-commerce and social media landscape, you will have to experiment more in China than in your home market.

Section Three

How Fast Can You Run?—for people
who are growing nicely in China

10

Holidays And Digital Promotion Strategies

As China is the most important cross-border e-commerce market in the world, brands of all sizes, small or large, have the opportunity to reach Chinese consumers when they are at the most engaged, playing games or buying items or engaging with brands on 11.11.

—Hendrik Laubscher, CEO and
Chief Analyst, Blue Cape Ventures[*]

Although retailers around the world build their campaigns around holidays, China is more oriented toward holidays and promotions than any other major market. Indeed, China is the first market to promote a holiday for the sole purpose of online shopping: Singles' Day. This one holiday accounts for close to 5 per cent of all e-commerce sales in China[†and‡] and on the Alibaba platform it reaches almost 8 per cent. For comparison, the largest online sales day in the US,[§] Cyber Monday, accounts for some 2 per cent of total annual US online retail sales.[¶]

Planning your sales calendar around the Chinese retail holiday calendar is essential. First, there is a mutually reinforcing phenomenon of

---

[*] https://alibaba.brand.live/c/11-11
[†] https://www.qianzhan.com/analyst/detail/220/201119-931dc80b.html
[‡] https://data.stats.gov.cn/easyquery.htm?cn=A01
[§] https://www.cnbc.com/2020/12/01/holiday-2020-shoppers-spend-10point8-billion-on-cyber-monday.html
[¶] https://www.census.gov/retail/mrts/www/data/pdf/ec_current.pdf

consumers chasing bargains and merchants offering them. The signals to the market could not be clearer.

Second, there is widespread institutional and platform advertising and promotion activity to drive purchasing. So the platforms themselves offer prizes and loyalty points, beyond store-level activity.

Third, this is an example of crowd behavior, meaning that shopping is not just socially acceptable but socially desirable. You must be able to tell your friends that you participated. As noted in Chapter 7, China consumer behavior is motivated by collective norms and collective experience. You cannot be absent from the game.

In sum, shopping booms on holidays because the merchants offer the best deals, the platforms have the best promotions, and all of your friends and relatives are shopping too.

In this chapter, we make the transition from the big picture discussion of platforms and social media we explored in the previous chapter to a more in-depth look at how businesses can craft the perfect China marketing plan—starting with holidays and exploring how you can stay successful and digitally relevant all year long. Then we take a deep dive into Singles' Day,

The Three Big Shopping Holidays and the Rest

As in other countries, some holidays are official government holidays, similar to July 4; some are cultural, similar to Halloween or St Patrick's Day; some are essentially holidays for gift-giving, similar to Valentine's Day.

In China, the three largest shopping holidays are June 18, November 11, and December 12, widely known as 6.18, 11.11, and 12.12.

6.18: China's June 18 shopping festival was started by JD in 2004 but has since grown as other platforms like Alibaba and Pinduoduo have joined the promotion. It is now the second-largest shopping day in China.

11.11: November 11 is the largest, busiest, and most consequential shopping day in the world: Singles' Day. Notably, Alibaba broadened the sales day this year to add November 1–3 to the original November 11 sales day. These three extra days drive higher sales numbers and take some of the pressure off the national logistics system.

12.12: Double 12, the less glamorous younger brother perhaps, but still vital to a serious China strategy. Its main value, explained below, is as a backstop for an 11.11 strategy.

We estimate that these three sales days together account for over 15 per cent of national e-commerce sales.

In addition, merchants should be aware of other holidays.

China's Valentine's Day. Known as the Qixi Festival, it celebrates romantic love and typically lands in August, actually on the seventh day of the seventh lunar month.

Lunar New Year Festival, often referred to as Chinese New Year. Typically, in February and the largest travel holiday in the world, as it is based around family gatherings.

Mid-Autumn Festival, or the Mooncake Festival, typically in September. Both the Lunar New Year and the mid-Autumn Festival are filled with gift-giving to family members and colleagues. Many of popular presents include fruit, candy, snacks and money.

Men are also known to buy gifts for women on International Women's Day (March 8).

National Day (October 1) is part of a holiday week, Golden Week, the first week of October.

Other large-scale celebrations in China include Labour Day (May 1), and the Dragon Boat Festival, (also in May).

These holidays aren't all major gift-giving days, but sites and platforms do attract individual buyers due to discounts and promotions—much like the sales found on August 8th (8.8) and September 9th (9.9), two days that signify luck in Chinese culture.

In sum, your opportunities around holidays and promotions will be a blend of cultural norms, official government holidays, and platform merchandising—not really a different mix than what you might find in western countries, but a more powerful mix in China.

Chinese Holidays

Here is an overview of the Chinese calendar cycle and gift-giving traditions. Some of the traditional holidays follow the lunar calendar and the official holidays tend to follow the western calendar.

Jan.–Feb.: Chinese New Year—Gift giving? Yes.

Feb. 14: Western Valentine's Day—Gift giving? Yes.

March 8: International Women's Day—Gift giving? Yes.

April: QingMing Festival (Tomb-Sweeping Day)—Gift giving? To leave at the graves of the departed.

May 1: Labour Day—Gift giving? No.

May: Dragon Boat Festival—Gift giving? No.

June 18: Summer Sales—Gift giving? No.

August: QiXi Festival (Chinese Valentine's Day)—Gift giving? Yes.

Oct. 1–7: National Day; Golden Week—Gift giving? No

Nov. 11: Singles' Day—Gift giving? No.

Dec. 12: Double 12—Gift giving? No.

Dec. 25: Christmas—Gift giving? Yes.

The biggest of these is Singles' Day

Singles' Day no longer just adds to your China strategy; it is the culmination of your China strategy. It defines consumer behavior and brand strategy in the market. Brands can spend six to eight months planning their Singles' Day activity.

	Alibaba annual retail GMV (billion RMB)	Alibaba Singles' Day GMV (billion RMB)	Percentage
2014	1578	57·1	4%
2015	2444	91·2	4%
2016	3092	120·7	4%
2017	3767	168·2	4%

2018	4820	213.5	4%
2019	5727	268.4	5%
2020	6589	498.2	8%

Alibaba's Singles' Day sales passed US$74.1 billion and JD's sales were US$41 billion, making it the biggest shopping stretch in the world, offline or online.* China sells more online during Singles' Day than most countries do in a year, with only the United States, Japan, and the UK selling more in a year than China sells during this one holiday.

Singles' Day Deep Dive

Singles' Day started as a campus social activity at Nanjing University in 1993, allowing unmarried singles to celebrate their status. Alibaba adopted this as a Tmall shopping day in 2009. The rationale is that, somewhat like western countries and Japan, China faces demographic trends that work against gift-giving and celebrations: smaller families, fewer children, later marriages, and more people living alone, in other words more singles. Singles' Day was therefore conceived as a good day for a singles' party or maybe a blind date. Alibaba's first year with Singles' Day in 2009 was a somewhat lonely affair, with twenty-seven merchants participating and sales of US$7.6 million GMV.†

The commercial logic of Singles' Day is that you don't have to wait for a gift to enjoy something new or exciting. If you always wanted a big-screen TV, this is the time to buy it. This spirit is captured by a Chinese saying, 'If you cannot be with someone you like, you can at least be with some*thing* you like.'

In 2020, Singles' Day solidified its status as the world's biggest shopping event, a far cry from its early days which involved only a handful of merchants. Never before in Chinese history had consumers had so much purchasing power, and Alibaba helped provide them with a place to go, and promoted a holiday to celebrate their purchases. Also, note that

---

* https://www.cnbc.com/2020/11/12/singles-day-2020-alibaba-and-jd-rack-up-record-115-billion-of-sales.html

† https://alibaba.brand.live/c/11-11

the platforms extended Singles' Day to extra days, with Alibaba adding November 1–3 in addition to November 11. Other platforms had similar additions, partially to keep the powerful sales day going and partially to reduce logistics pressure.

At Alibaba:

- 11.11 sales grew 26 per cent over the previous year and reached US$75 billion GMV.[*]
- The most popular countries for imported products were the United States, Australia, Canada, France, Germany, Italy, Japan, Korea, New Zealand, and the UK.
- There were over 800 million consumers; 2,50,000 brands, with 31,000 of them overseas brands.
- Over 470 brands surpassed RMB100 Million (US$14.9 Million) in GMV, including Adidas, Apple, Estée Lauder, L'Oréal, Lancôme and Nike.
- Michael Kors's sales earnings broke over $100 million, and Cartier sold a $28 million necklace during a livestream event witnessed by almost 8,00,000 people.[†]

At JD:

- 11.11 sales grew 32 per cent YoY and reached US$41 billion GMV.[‡]
- The most popular countries for imported products were the United States, Japan, and Germany.[§]
- 264 brands saw over RMB100 million in sales, and over 13,000 brands saw their sales double.[¶]

---

[*] https://www.chinainternetwatch.com/31334/double-11-2020/

[†] https://jingdaily.com/china-singles-day-luxury-brands-record-sales-lvmh-prada/

[‡] https://www.chinainternetwatch.com/31334/double-11-2020/

[§] https://jdcorporateblog.com/jd-reports-to-record-rmb-271-5-billion-singles-day-performance-2/

[¶] https://jdcorporateblog.com/in-depth-singles-day-carnival-shows-jds-power-to-boosts-real-economy/

- The top five selling brands were Apple, Sony, Siemens, Philips and Panasonic.[*]
- JD's imported goods supermarket saw turnover increase 2.5 times month-on-month.
- 93 per cent of orders were delivered to customers in twenty-four hours.

There are several reasons for this success.

Consumerism as entertainment: Pre-COVID, Tmall hosted a national television gala on November 10 with a countdown to the midnight start of Singles' Day that gave New Year's Eve at Times Square a run for its money. This is the Hollywood-style spectacle we foreshadowed in Chapter 1, with loads of international stars and an audience of 200 million viewers. Consumerism is enhanced by group behavior and it is an entertainment channel as well. In 2020, the gala was virtual, and was augmented by product launch events, live-stream shows, fan contests and demonstrations.

We mentioned David Beckham and Taylor Swift in Chapter 1, and other international celebrities who participated in Singles' Day 2020 events included basketball icon Magic Johnson, and singer Katy Perry. In the past, basketball legend Kobe Bryant, singer Mariah Carey, social media celebrity Kim Kardashian, model Miranda Kerr, actress Scarlett Johansson, actress Nicole Kidman, and singer Pharrell Williams also joined in.[†and‡]

It is not just Alibaba: JD, PDD, and other platforms are jumping in as well. If you are selling on JD or other platforms, you will also see a full range of promotional activity, albeit on a smaller scale.

The Platforms set the rules, and the rules favor the consumers: Tmall and JD have established a virtuous cycle of collective consumerism. If a brand wants to participate in the Singles' Day promotion, offering the lowest pricing is mandatory. Inventory must also be guaranteed (back

---

[*] https://jdcorporateblog.com/jd-reports-to-record-rmb-271-5-billion-singles-day-performance-2/

[†] https://www.cbsnews.com/news/chinese-shoppers-spend-over-100-billion-in-shopping-fest/

[‡] https://radiichina.com/kim-kardashian-west-livestream/

orders are not possible). So every Chinese consumer knows they will receive the best price possible. Even if you do not watch US football every week, you try to follow the Super Bowl. Even if you are not much of a shopper, you try to buy something on Singles' Day.

Good gets better: Expect an ongoing expansion of two key trends: new markets and omnichannel. In new markets, Singles' Day has caught on in Taiwan, Hong Kong, and Singapore and is starting to see traction in Southeast Asia. In omnichannel, which we discussed in-depth in Chapter 8, Alibaba and JD have each made major strides in integrating their online system with their offline footprint. You might start with only a Tmall store, but you could quickly add on offline distribution as the major retail chains look to Tmall results when taking on a new brand.

Scale: 11.11 transaction volume is large enough to drive both brand strategy and consumer behavior. 11.11 no longer augments your China strategy; it is your China strategy.

Engagement: Don't lose sight of the other main goal for Singles' Day. It is not just a day for transactions; it is a day to engage the consumer. 11.11 is a chance to speak to China consumers, whether you are introducing a new product or refreshing your brand. There are plenty of sales and bargains, but the day is much more than a celebration of mark-downs. You are joining the national conversation. You need to have something to say. Some brands will launch products specifically for Singles' Day. Others will offer live-streamed contests and reality TV shows. According to Alibaba President Michael Evans:

> Of course the big businesses, the Estée Lauders, the Apples, the Nikes, they've done extremely well. But as you know one of our big focuses this year was small businesses . . . And whether it's Uncle Bud and the live streaming from brand partner Magic Johnson, or Bisell, or Allbirds, or Pipette or Fender or C.O. Bigelow . . . this was a huge focus for us this year because we wanted to show that with technology, and with focus, the China market is open to everybody not just the big guys, but to the little guys, as well.[*]

---

[*] https://alibaba.brand.live/c/11-11

It is the future of digital innovation: In 2020, Alibaba and JD gave out coupons in exchange for people playing their online games.* In the past, Tmall featured an augmented reality game to allow people to chase black cats—the Tmall mascot—like *Pokémon GO*. Tmall has also unveiled for the sale a virtual reality shopping experience that allows consumers to connect their smartphones with a VR headset and make purchases as if they were in a physical store in New York City. And there are mobile apps that enable shoppers to digitally see how they look in clothes and cosmetics.

Prime Day vs Singles' Day

How does Amazon's Prime Day compare to Alibaba's Singles' Day? These two extravaganzas are not just carbon copies; each has its distinctive architecture and strategy, reflecting differences in both the two markets they serve as well as in the two companies.

What's similar

Scale: Each event is a large-scale shopping holiday built around high volume, deep discounts and thin margins.

Multi-market: Amazon has added Australia, the Netherlands and Singapore to its list of participating countries. Alibaba has further integrated its Lazada acquisition to add Thailand, Malaysia, Indonesia, Vietnam, Singapore and the Philippines.

Omnichannel: Amazon will bring its Whole Foods subsidiary into Prime Day, while Alibaba has integrated its Intime Department Stores and Hema shops, allowing both platforms to reach consumers who are more comfortable with offline than online.

---

* https://www.scmp.com/abacus/tech/article/3108768/singles-day-mini-games-keep-shoppers-coming-back-more-taobao-and-jdcom

What's somewhat similar

Multimedia: Both have offline events to bolster online sales. As mentioned earlier, Tmall runs a nationally televised gala in China as a countdown activity. Amazon started running offline events in multiple cities for the first time. But the similarity ends there. Alibaba has made shopping entertaining and brought in a Hollywood production team to bolster its A-list. You can click to purchase while you watch the gala. You can use VR headsets to play games during the show. Shopping is fully integrated into the event. Amazon is built to be transactional; Tmall is built to be engaging. In other words, Singles' Day is a celebration. Prime Day is an online sale.

What's different

Size: In 2020, Singles' Day GMV reached $74·1 billion,[*] while Prime Day sales were $10·4 billion.[†]

Strategy: Singles' Day is brand-focused, Prime Day is Amazon-focused. Tmall has no 'ticket price' or paid membership. But Prime Day requires you to join Amazon Prime to participate. This reflects a difference in strategy: Tmall is trying to sell to the entire nation. Amazon is trying to reach its core e-commerce shoppers.

The Fourth Quarter—Your China Strategy?

In most countries, the fourth quarter is the most important period of the sales year, but no place more so than in China, where it is common for consumer brands to reach over 50 per cent of their annual sales in that ninety-day window. In that quarter, 11.11 is recognized as the most

---

[*] https://www.cnbc.com/2020/11/12/singles-day-2020-alibaba-and-jd-rack-up-record-115-billion-of-sales.html

[†] https://www.digitalcommerce360.com/article/amazon-prime-day-data/

important shopping day, but let's make sure attention is also given to 12.12, or Double 12.

Think about how the 11.11 shopping day was originally constructed. There is at least one big problem with 11.11. If you limit your activity to those twenty-four hours, you eventually bump against capacity constraints. Even if you heavy-up your warehouse and shipping, there is only so much that can be pumped through the system. Alibaba has partially solved this by making Singles' Day more of a season. As mentioned earlier, they added Nov. 1–3 to the original Nov. 11 sales day. Then they start 11.11 thirty days early and finish it thirty days late.

Thirty days before 11.11, you start to see teasers, special promotions, and lead-up events. And 11.11 keeps going for thirty days after leading to 12.12, the other shopping day. 12.12 also allows merchants to fully load inventory for 11.11, knowing they can move slower moving stock a month later with the next holiday.

In other words, one requirement for success in this quarter is for brands to take a holistic approach. Do not view these ninety days as a series of one-off events, but adopt an integrated strategy involving creativity and planning to ensure your opportunities build on each other: How do you rise above the noise and acquire consumers already loyal to a competitor? How do you retain your existing base?

Here are four lessons from the fourth quarter to frame the role of innovation and planning, reminding us of the central roles that 11.11 and 12.12 play in the process:

Treat Singles' Day as More Than a 'Day'

To fuel Singles' Day excitement, Alibaba introduced a 'pre-sale' period that begins in late October. This gives brands the opportunity to engage with consumers well before the holiday. Estée Lauder, as an example, produced an ad campaign using celebrities, Li Xian and Yang Mi, to promote its Aqua Brilliance line. The campaign was shot in the desert, highlighting the strength of the product's moisturizing effect and conveying a message of no issues with cracked or dry skin even in the harshest of climates. This innovative '11.11 Pre-Sale' campaign helped Estée Lauder generate over

$70 million in sales in less than an hour and was launched weeks before the official holiday.

If the pre-sale campaign starts in October, you need to sign up with Tmall by September, and goods might have to be in place by September 1, so your operational/inventory components have to be determined over the summer.

Use 12.12 as a Strategic Backstop for 11.11

Sometimes brands build their fourth quarter strategy around 11.11, without fully taking on board the value of 12.12. December 12 serves as another super-promotion day. But what is the utility of having two shopping days so close together? Won't consumers and merchants be fatigued, and won't immediate consumer demand be satisfied?

Perhaps, but there are counterarguments. For the brands, 12.12 allows them to overshoot on 11.11 in terms of inventory and experimentation, with the knowledge that 12.12 can be used to absorb any surplus and keep any successful experiments in play. In other words, 12.12 gives you a longer tail to your sales curve with enough of a breather to allow you to adjust for market conditions.

For the consumers, satisfaction can spur demand rather than satiate it. In other words, a successful product launch can lead to word-of-mouth, broader consumer acceptance, and a spill-over effect in the market. In my experience, 12.12 sales should track at 20 per cent to 25 per cent of 11.11 sales.

Think Beyond Discounts

Traditionally, super promotion days (11.11, 12.12) were events for consumers to get up to 50 per cent off the retail price of a product. This type of discount is still the norm, but there's been a recent wave of additional incentives: exclusive Singles' Day branded product sets, fan contests such as a raffle to win a trip to a brand's global HQ, and even exclusive offline events such as spend a certain amount and earn a ticket to Shanghai's Fashion Show. Beyond the L'Oréal case study in Chapter 5, the brand also partnered with KOL Austin Li—China's 'lipstick king'—in a one-hour livestream that took place on 11.11. Austin was joined by actor Zhuyi Long, who helped L'Oréal to sell-through over 10,000 units of its star product, a skin rejuvenating serum.

Connect Global with Local

For international brands that demand a premium price point, the bar for acquiring and retaining customers continues to rise. Customers want to know they are receiving international quality, but they also want the sense that the brand is identifying with their needs and wants at a local level. To connect the global with the local, beauty conglomerate Lancôme displayed branded spotlights upon iconic landmarks, including the Eiffel Tower and Shanghai's Global Harbor. To bring its product formulations to China at a local level, Lancôme also held events titled 'Expo of the Rose' in Nanjing, Chengdu and other cities to educate consumers on the benefits of its rose-based essential oils.

In sum, Singles' Day represents innovation, growth, and opportunity in China e-commerce. Brands that make full use of all the promotional opportunities, and who view them as components of an integrated campaign have the most to gain.

Key Takeaways

> Holidays and promotions drive consumer behavior in China more so than in other markets. Brands need to stay digitally relevant during these special periods and adjust to the Chinese holiday schedule.

> Singles' Day is the largest shopping extravaganza in the world, and it unfolds over sixty days or so, with planning starting months before.

11

Risk and Compliance

Managing the Unknown. Not Every Day is a Sunny Day.

The goal is to manage risk, not to eliminate it completely. If you wait for perfect conditions, you will face perfect competition.

There are two things no business likes: surprise and change. Businesses want a stable, predictable operating environment so they can get on with, well, business. This probably sums up why many businesses do not venture into a new market, be it China or the market next door. Every market in the world has a different commercial environment, with different competitors and different consumers leading to different commercial outcomes.

But beyond those different commercial circumstances, every market also has a different risk and regulatory profile. This chapter will discuss those China requirements so that you can ensure your strategy is designed to deal with the possible twists, from currency movements to intellectual piracy.

Let's break the risk down into three general categories: commercial, regulatory, and political risks.

1. **Commercial risk:** Most businesses understand this phenomenon even if they don't like it much. We all know a business can suffer if its products are not taken up in the market, if sales were overestimated, or

if a new competitor enters. Beyond that product-specific commercial risk, there is macro commercial risk. The business cycle still exists, and economies are subject to slow downs—even occasionally contracting. Currency movements are in this category

2. **Regulatory risk**: This involves intellectual property (IP) issues such as trademarks and copyrights, including IP theft. It also involves compliance issues such as testing and labelling. Finally, there are legal obligations in areas such as tax and labor law.

3. **Other compliance issues**: The regulatory framework in China is likely to be different than in your home market, in everything from product testing to severance pay.

4. **Political risk**: This can be a new area for businesses. What does trade friction and the possibility of new tariffs mean? What if issues with my country spill over and infect consumer preferences?

5. **Systemic shocks**: What will you do when the next pandemic strikes?

While the bad—or perhaps daunting—news is that these problems are real possibilities, the good news is that there are steps you can take to greatly reduce or eliminate their likelihood or their costs; all of which we will be discussing in the sections below.

Risk One: Commercial Risk

Although China's economy is on a nice post-COVID rebound in 2021, with the World Bank projecting 7.9 per cent growth,* I continue to hear questions from merchants who do business or are considering doing business in China. They are wondering about how an economic slowdown might affect sales, of course, but they are also concerned about stock market volatility, China's reform plans, currency stability and myriad other uncertainties.

Underlying all is a more fundamental question: How can a business make plans when the economic road ahead is shrouded in fog and the

---

* https://www.worldbank.org/en/news/press-release/2021/01/05/global-economy-to-expand-by-4-percent-in-2021-vaccine-deployment-and-investment-key-to-sustaining-the-recovery

possibility of bad economic news seems to lurk around every corner? A commercial risk strategy helps you get through uncertain times.

This is not specific to China. Any rational business poised to enter any new market is going to ask the same questions. Effective business strategy often hinges on predictability. We all crave the familiar and we can more easily build our projections and goals when we are operating in known territory.

Unfortunately, new market entry is by definition a bit of a journey into the unknown. So at the start, a company has to develop a consensus that it will be able to tolerate a greater degree of variability in results when playing away games than it experiences at home. Uncertainty is more a part of your life when you enter a new market than when you simply stay in your home market.

China isn't Ohio, no question. But during uncertain times and in uncharted waters, there are steps you can take to position your company to succeed regardless of geography and current economic conditions.

First, understand that commercial growth is usually not highly correlated with economic growth. Consumer spending tends to outpace overall economic activity, especially in emerging markets, which means your sales growth should outperform GDP growth—and many consumer products regularly do. So even with a maturing economy and some tapering of historically high growth rate, China will likely continue to see solid growth in the retail sector for years to come. The simple reason is that people want a better life, and consumer goods help provide it.

Here are three steps you can take in China to mitigate commercial risk:

1. Adopt a flexible, scalable model, with a low break-even. From the outset, you might want to sacrifice some efficiency to reduce your cost structure by, for example, heavily outsourcing for the first few years while you establish your market position.
2. Be cautious about taking on debt and fixed costs. Even if your home market model calls for you to operate your own fleet of trucks, better to lease trucks or—even better—outsource delivery activities in China. If you normally build your own warehouse on the assumption

you will hit $30 million in sales, instead try leasing a warehouse for a year or two until you are certain you will reach that target. The golden rule for any new market is, be wary of debt. You might not have the volume to service it. There is always the prospect for volatility in the marketplace and the laws of economics apply in China as they do elsewhere. Foreign businesses should be mindful of fixed costs and tilt as much as possible to a variable cost model.

3. Have a currency strategy. You do not need to predict currency movements, but you do need to adjust to them as quickly as possible. You might find in the course of a long-term currency shift that your product is now mis-priced in the market. For example, you based your model around listing your product for RMB 200 because that was close to your home market price. But after an ongoing currency shift, there is now a divergence between two prices. Worse, this means your profitability is now in question. The simple solution here is to regularly monitor and adjust prices. Your CFO needs to monitor the RMB exchange rate, the same way the CFO might monitor fuel prices or other inputs in your business.

Fortunately, e-commerce allows you to deal successfully with all three elements. It is a scalable model, with no in-country assets beyond inventory and very little in the way of fixed costs. Additionally, prices can be adjusted daily, so there is little in the way of currency exposure.

E-commerce provides the most cost-effective way to enter or to compete in the market, rain or shine. A flagship store can frequently be set up on Tmall for about $100,000, including deposit, registration, trademark registration, product testing and approval, web page design and set up, warehouse operations, and CRM training. This is a dramatic reduction in market-entry costs compared with setting up brick-and-mortar shops, and as a result, the break-even point is much lower online than offline.

Any new market entry strategy demands the flexibility to operate in an unpredictable environment. China is no different in this regard, but because of geographical distance and language gaps, foreign firms tend to have less familiarity with this market, and often a lower comfort level. E-commerce can instill confidence by reducing complexity, costs, and time-to-market, giving companies the room to succeed in good times and bad.

Risk Two: Regulatory Risk and Compliance

One of the historic challenges in China is the problem of counterfeits and intellectual property (IP) rights. Within China, there have been cases of entirely fake retail stores (encountered by Apple); suppliers and manufacturers producing products after hours to sell as original (encountered by Nike and Budweiser); and the production of pirated Madonna compact discs on Army bases. Even though these examples have been cleaned up, the scale and brazenness of IP theft in China colors how many retail brands approach the market. It is perhaps unfair to lay these structural problems at the feet of e-commerce, but it is easy to see why brands are concerned.

There has been substantial improvement in the China IP environment in recent years, especially for retail goods. One of the more important: Alibaba, JD, and PDD each have on-line take down procedures through which brands can complain and have pirated goods removed. Here are five additional steps companies can take:

1. **Do Your Homework:** Businesses that plan to enter China should register trademarks with the China Trademark Office as soon as possible. Register both your home country name as well as your Chinese name. According to Maarten Roos, a leading international IP attorney in Shanghai, registration

    . . . . . . is the very first step to ensure that one's IP rights are actually protected under Chinese law.*

Because China has a 'first-to-file' system for trademarks and patents, the registration of such products and marks is open to third parties. Michael Jordan, for example, owns the trademark to his name and accompanying

---

* https://www.linkedin.com/pulse/selling-china-five-steps-protect-your-intellectual-property-lavin

brands in the US, but at first did not have ownership in China of its Chinese translation. It took eight years of litigation in China, resulting in a favorable 2020 ruling from the Supreme People's Court, for Jordan to win the rights to his name.[*]

2. **Get in the Game**: The best defense is a strong offense. This means you need to start actively selling in the market. The easier it is for consumers to find authentic products, the more difficult it is for pirates to sell counterfeit goods. Pirates are opportunistic and will take advantage of slower-moving firms. We have found that upwards of 50 per cent of pirated goods disappear when the product is made legally available. Make the legal leap and open an e-commerce store.

3. **Keep Your Guard Up**: If China IP is more challenging than any other market in the world, the response needs to be stronger than any other market in the world. Complaining about a problem is not a strategy. Indignation is not a plan. Brands must actively manage their IP assets.

- Monitor on-line sites to ensure all products are legitimate.
- Use a secret shopper program to test the authenticity of products.
- Consider adding anti-counterfeiting codes to products so that consumers can confirm authenticity, a measure currently used by Elizabeth Arden and Shiseido.
- Make full use of loyalty and affinity programs to increase the value of the official product.

4. **Develop a Response**: Track, report, complain, and follow-up. There are various legal and administrative steps companies can take if their IP rights have been infringed, among them:

- Use the take-down mechanism offered by the platform. The major platforms take these complaints seriously.
- Work with an attorney to send a cease-and-desist letter to the infringer.

---

[*] https://www.si.com/nba/2020/04/14/michael-jordan-copyright-lawsuit-case-china

- File a complaint with administrative authorities, typically the Administration for Industry and Commerce or the Intellectual Property Office.
- File a civil lawsuit.
- File a complaint with the local Public Security Bureau, but remember this office handles trademark infringements only.
- Register trademarks with Customs, allowing officers to note IP infringements during routine inspections and notify the IP owner.

While the legal infrastructure for IP infringements is improving, Roos stresses the importance of having a

> . . . strategy in place to minimize the damage that infringements do to a brand name.[*]

5. **Work with Your Partners**: You need friends. Brands can enhance their effectiveness in combating IP issues by working with like-minded institutions, such as trade associations, chambers of commerce, embassies, domestic and international law firms, as well as e-commerce service providers. It is important to recognize that many other brands face similar challenges and have different areas of expertise. Your company may need to reach outside its internal corporate capabilities to expand its situational awareness and better address IP issues.

We recommend a mix of the above tactics, customized for the challenge at hand. Businesses that are accustomed to mature market conditions might be frustrated by the imperfections in China's market. In our experience, however, we have found that almost all imperfections have solutions. It is okay to complain, but we have to do more than *only* complain.

Risk Three: Other Compliance issues

There are other important compliance issues beyond intellectual property:

---

[*] https://www.linkedin.com/pulse/selling-china-five-steps-protect-your-intellectual-property-lavin

Grey market or parallel imports: Every company has a different view of grey market activity. Initially, it can help build demand, but as brands mature in the market, they tend to be more concerned about product quality and adulteration as well as price competition. Grey markets can lead to customer confusion, channel conflicts, and IP challenges. In China, you will probably need a grey market strategy similar to your IP strategy

Testing and Labelling: These requirements in China are similar to those in other markets. Cosmetics—anything that touches the skin—must be tested. Food items—anything that is ingested—must be tested. Clothing and apparel must be tested. And all these items must be labelled as well. The good news is that products sold through the cross-border model do not have to meet any of these requirements as they do not enter the market until after they are sold.

Tax and Labor issues: The other general corporate issues are also non-existent with the cross-border model because the platform collects the taxes for the government. You have no labor issues because you have no employees in-country. Of course, if you decide to establish an in-country organization you will need to develop internal and external resources to recruit, hire, and manage local employees in compliance with national and regional labor laws. This will probably require working with a Chinese intermediary company or an International PEO (Professional Employer Organization).

Risk Four: Political Risk

The China-US trade relationship is one of the largest in the world, with China being typically the US's third-largest trading relationship, behind Canada and Mexico, and the US being China's largest or second-largest trading partner, sometimes behind the EU. Every day, consumers and companies in both the United States and China find their lives improved because of access to better variety and less expensive products.

Nonetheless, size doesn't eliminate problems. As trade grows and economies become more complex, there are bound to be issues. China has long limited US companies from competing in various sectors, even as Chinese products enjoy generally open access to the American market. This asymmetry has pushed the China trade agenda front and center in Washington. There is a widespread view in the US that China has not been even-handed in its trade relations with the United States and this unfairness obligates the US to push back. During the Trump Administration, this resulted in the US imposing a range of tariffs on China, with China responding by imposing tariffs on the US.

Retail hope: As one who has spent much of his professional life involved in the US–China trade policy, I must confess that I generally share the US perspective that it is more difficult for a US company to sell into China than for a Chinese company to sell into the US. The business climate in China can be challenging for Americans and the joint rise of nationalism in China and economic populism in the United States creates additional risks.

But I hasten to add, the retail sector is one of the bright spots in the trade relationship, perhaps the brightest. Not only are American exports of consumer goods growing, but the regulatory environment on the China side is actually improving, with strong growth in the cross-border segment of that market. Simply put, China's cross-border regulations allow any international brand to sell its products into China without going through a sometimes expensive regulatory and labelling procedure. As discussed in Chapters 8 and 9, both Alibaba and JD have captured this market segment by establishing special cross-border channels, Tmall Global and JD Worldwide, and putting in place a world-class logistics solution.

So cross-border success is not by accident; it is by design. China has liberalized this segment purposefully, not as a loophole. It is easy to see why China is comfortable when it comes to retail growth.

First, Chinese firms such as Alibaba, JD, and PDD dominate the e-commerce ecosystem, so regardless of from where the goods might come, the China side will still profit. As I tell friends from these companies when they ask about my business, Export Now is a feeder airline. Our entire business model is to bring international goods to the Chinese platforms. Companies such as Export Now do not compete with the Chinese platforms, they make it easier for the mid-tier brands to sell on the platforms, thereby creating a win-win-win outcome in which the platform, the brand, and Export Now all come out ahead.

Second, consumer goods are not viewed as strategic, like banks or telecoms, so if a US cosmetic brand gains market share, this is not a troubling development.

Third, over time, Chinese firms will increasingly develop the ability to compete in foreign markets as well, a practice we are already seeing as Alipay expands to the United States and Europe.

The bottom line: Keep these points in mind as you hear more about US–China trade issues.

- Trade issues are going to receive more attention from the US Government and there is a likelihood of increased public comment and even friction. Steel, in particular, is a sore spot for the United States, with a broad view that the US steel industry faces unfair competition from overseas markets, including China
- Both sides have shown to date a capacity to manage these issues without them spilling over into an all-out trade war. Even at the peak of tension during the Trump Administration, the Chinese government never called for a boycott of American goods.
- Historically, consumer goods and e-commerce have been a shining example of bilateral cooperation and neither side has sought to undermine or impede this success.

Risk Five: Systemic Shocks

Whether your business is grappling with Brexit implications for UK inventory, or Australian brush fire impacts on sales forecasting, it is a world of uncertainty. Let's take a look at how China handled COVID in 2020 to draw some general conclusions about crisis management.

Is it possible to venture into China in the middle of a major disruption such as the 2020 coronavirus storm? Can a business still operate in the world's second-largest economy even with the possibilities of lockdowns, closed factories, and even entire cities being placed under quarantine?

China's market was battered in early 2020 as the number of confirmed cases shot up and strict measures were adopted to bring the outbreak under control. Fortunately, these measures resulted in China getting its arms around the pandemic more quickly than many other countries, and a quick return to business as usual—with one important exception.

Consumer behavior in China through the pandemic

Consumer activity normally freezes during Chinese New Year as millions of people travel and spend time with their families. Most businesses are shut down. Because of the coronavirus, the Chinese government extended the 2020 New Year's holiday for a second week and many locales, such as Shanghai, extended it a third week. In my view, these extra holidays were the right decision, but this resulted in a near collapse of consumer spending in February. People don't buy when they are away from home.

Beyond the holiday shut-down, a turmoil alters consumer behavior. People pull back from spending during uncertainty. Purchases of necessities continue, but big-ticket items are deferred. Car sales in China were down 80 per cent in February 2020, with the major companies suspending production.

Location-dependent industries such as food and beverage, Shanghai Disneyland, and the hotel industry were in for longer-term bad news as people minimized their travel, similar to the patterns we saw in the US and Europe.

What is working?

As the storm in China began to abate, there was a solid uptick in China consumer behavior as early as March. It is worth highlighting a few of the strengths in the Chinese retail segment.

Necessities: We see a sustained improvement in demand for groceries and personal care products, with apparel holding its own.

E-commerce: This is the exception to business as usual. COVID brought some permanent changes in retail goods: among consumers globally, COVID means a permanent shift to e-commerce. COVID also means non-traditional online shoppers, such as the very old and the very young, are now empowered and are comfortable with on-line activity. Digital is increasingly a way of life, a necessity.

This McKinsey survey shows how consumer activities in China were affected by COVID,*

With a general uptick in digital activities in areas from e-commerce to remote learning.

Pick-up of digital & low-touch activities during and after COVID-19[1]

% of respondents who replied using more or just started using

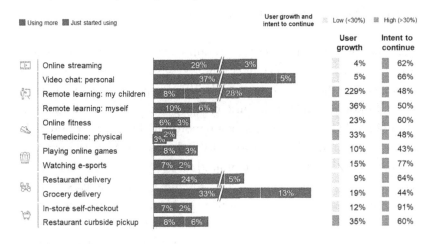

	User growth	Intent to continue
Online streaming	4%	62%
Video chat: personal	5%	66%
Remote learning: my children	229%	48%
Remote learning: myself	36%	50%
Online fitness	23%	60%
Telemedicine: physical	33%	48%
Playing online games	10%	43%
Watching e-sports	15%	77%
Restaurant delivery	9%	64%
Grocery delivery	19%	44%
In-store self-checkout	12%	91%
Restaurant curbside pickup	35%	60%

[1]Q: Have you used or done any of the following since the COVID-19 situation started? If yes, Q: Which best describes when you have done or used each of these items? Possible answers: "just started using since COVID-19 started"; "using more since COVID-19 started"; "using about the same since COVID-19 started"; "using less since COVID-19 started."

Source: McKinsey COVID-19 China Consumer Pulse Survey

Financial support: The 'dog that didn't bark' during COVID was China's financial sector. China was determined to see that the public health emergency did not become a broader economic disaster. China's central bank lowered rates and pumped in liquidity, similar to actions taken in Europe and the United States. Domestic banks were given leeway on loans, and there were other initiatives similar to what western countries implemented. Although there will no doubt be economic damage because of the coronavirus, the interesting story is how well the economy has held up. Consumer confidence is on the rebound. One data point: The

---

* https://www.mckinsey.com/business-functions/marketing-and-sales/our-insights/survey-chinese-consumer-sentiment-during-the-coronavirus-crisis

Shanghai Stock Exchange Composite Index was up 14 per cent for 2020. The economic turmoil brought on by COVID did not translate into broader financial market panic. Business confidence remained on track.

What this means for International Brands: Marketing lessons and management lessons

In marketing terms, I suggest three COVID lessons:

First, the fundamental value proposition of entering the China market remains intact. China is still China. China's consumers are still consuming. The economy, though off-peak, will be the best performing of the major world economies. Indeed, because of the global economic turmoil, for many brands China presents the best opportunity for growth world-wide.

Second, you should expect volatility in the market. You need a variable cost model. If you had pre-storm projections of $8 million in sales it might now only be $7 million. This drop in revenue might be a disaster if you were in bricks and mortar, but it is manageable if you are on-line.

Third, you need a longer time horizon. Success in China can easily take a few years, particularly if you are a new-to-market brand. You need a model that can withstand a bad month or even a bad quarter. You need to play for the long run.

Whether a pandemic, an economic shock, or a natural disaster, there are four management lessons:

First, make sure your China team is safe. Remember the human factor. Be flexible on working from home. Avoid unnecessary travel.

Second, increase your internal communications. Managers should check in with every employee and make sure their family situation is okay. Do they need food or other supplies? Do they have to take care of a relative? A little support goes a long way in a difficult moment.

Third, don't take any steps that might contribute to a sense of panic, even inadvertently. You might need to postpone some plans, but be thoughtful about how you announce it.

Fourth, be careful about pushing disaster messaging in your marketing. You want to avoid being seen as trying to take advantage of a bad situation. Focus on philanthropic initiatives.

There is certainly a lot of bad economic news in the world today, but in China's consumer segment at least, the good news outweighs the bad. 2020 was the best year ever for Alibaba, Pinduoduo, and JD. Which means it was a very good year for the leading brands on those platforms as well.

Compliance and Risk: Concluding Thoughts

Businesses looking at a China expansion or market entry will have to weigh the advantages of participating in this market with the additional element of uncertainty and potential risk. There are two ever-present dangers for foreign businesses in China. First, it is generally a mistake to try to do *everything*—to try to replicate the entire scope of your home market activity in China. It is a far greater mistake to do *nothing*—to allow an increase in uncertainty to prompt the company to freeze all China plans. A China strategy or a broader international strategy can actually reduce risk, by diversifying markets. Don't make the mistake of seeking a perfect, risk-free environment. If you wait for perfect conditions, you will face perfect competition. As I wrote in the prologue, don't stand still, but don't get swept up in bad news either.

In short, here are five quick tips to avoid missteps in China:

One: keep moving ahead with your business plans. No one likes partners who panic—not customers, suppliers, nor the Chinese government. By all means, adjust operations to market condition, but continue operations and keep on with your plans for growth. To falter or freeze in the face of bad news risks the perception you are contributing to the problem. The United States and China have had many ups and downs in their relationship, but over the past thirty years, trade problems have been short-term.

Two: your leadership needs to understand the China market will tend to have more volatility than the developed markets. Beyond the trade issues, commercial questions from consumer preferences to the competitive map are still being defined. China is a market of extraordinary possibilities and extraordinary fluctuation as well.

Three: bolster your communications and outreach activity. Your corporate web page explains your values and mission, but is it in the Chinese language? If you have a college internship program in the US, do you also have one in China? Pay attention to being a good corporate citizen and to ensuring Chinese constituencies understand what you do.

Four: don't forget internal constituencies. It might seem that everyone in your company is contacting you about a potential problem—why not get in front of the issue? I suggest regular internal emails or notices to your colleagues and collaborators to let them know that despite the public friction, day-to-day business continues to move ahead.

Five: strong partners in China are invaluable resources, not only in helping you market to Chinese customers, but also in navigating the sometimes-turbulent waters of regulation and compliance.

The bottom line: No market in the world offers the possibilities that China offers, and that can carry with it a certain number of challenges as well. It will require active management to surmount those challenges. The steps in this chapter are a nice start.

Key Takeaways

➤ Political issues and risk factors sometimes affect capital expenditure, big ticket items and financial instruments, but rarely affect consumer spending.

➤ Entering a new market can initially add a bit of volatility to a company's model as more unknowns are being introduced. However, the addition of multiple markets tends to decrease risk and volatility as the company benefits from diversification.

➤ The regulatory and compliance issues in China are similar to other markets but they can require an effort to get up to speed. New-to-market companies will likely want to pursue the simplest path initially to avoid over-complicating market entry. Fortunately, e-commerce offers a standard set of solutions for consumer goods.

12

The Art of Marketing in China

Chinese consumers are best understood as a connected network. They are constantly interacting and influencing each other. And what they say to each other about a brand is far more important than what the company says itself. KOLs and livestreaming are creatures of this consumer network. They are very good at influencing and activating such interactions.

—in conversation with Jeff Towson,
Professor, Beijing University

Much digital innovation has emerged catering to the evolving needs of the Chinese consumers. That process is accelerating as China enters into a new era of tech-enabled innovation epitomized by several key disruptive technologies that are manifesting commercially around the same time. They are the Internet-of-Things, artificial intelligence, cloud computing, 5G, and blockchain, riding on top of huge amounts of big data. As Chinese consumers' demand patterns for products and services continue to evolve, more opportunities and more innovations will also emerge.

—in conversation with Edward Tse,
Founder and CEO, Gao Feng Advisory

In many ways, marketing in China is similar to marketing in your home market. It's all about creating and communicating value to their targeted segments. Let's focus on how marketers communicate value.

You have to educate people, you have to create fun stories and ways for people to connect with the brand, and you have to stay in consumers' minds. You must funnel information, enjoyment, and social connectivity to your consumers.

Like at home, you'll have to make an investment to reach potential customers based on their demographics, psychographics, and behavior. Who are your customers? Where do they live? What are their interests? Which websites do they prefer?

The e-commerce platforms all sell a range of advertising products so that you can bid for key words or purchase adjacencies or banner ads. The Alibaba program, called Alimama, is regarded as the most versatile, but JD and PDD have their versions as well. In addition, you can seed off-platform by advertising on WeChat, Weibo and, if it's a luxury or beauty brand, Little Red Book—very similar to other countries.

But what is different in China? This chapter will discuss six elements of marketing communications in China that are different from your home market:

1. Marketing Collateral
2. Digital Reviews
3. Livestreaming
4. Social Promotions
5. Mini-Apps
6. Brand Collaboration

Marketing Collateral

The marketing collateral that works for you at home is not likely to work for you in China. The China audience wants content that is even more exciting, pertinent, culturally aware, and continual. This might be the fastest-moving market in the world in terms of marketing communications.

Before you enter China, you will need to think through the quantity and quality of your short videos, articles, photos and social media blasts.

- **Amount of material**—Right away, expect to be making at least one post a day. Many brands coming to China do not maintain a daily cadence in their home market, so this places extra demands on their creative and production team.

For the first few months, you might be able to largely use your home market content, translated and adapted. Over time you will learn additional modifications that work, from split tests and customer feedback.

- **Relevance of material**—Is your content considered new and on-point by Chinese consumers? For example, gardening or yard work is considered a worthy weekend hobby or activity in many western countries, but a home garden scene is unlikely to resonate with middle-class Chinese. A family scene with three kids? That is unlikely to work as well.
- **Cultural dimension of material**—Whether you hire an agency or rely on an in-house employee to help you to develop your digital marketing strategy, you should know your China audience and their cultural touch-points.

You can use western models to show the brand's authenticity, such as a Parisian model using French perfume, but then use Chinese models to show its workability and acceptance. Acknowledge your audience's culture and use of the product. Add subtitles, if needed. Your content must resonate with your new market.

Be politically aware. Statements that might be considered casual jokes in foreign markets might be viewed as political criticism in China. For instance, it's best to make sure you're putting Hong Kong into the right context on t-shirts.[*] Or forgo using chopsticks in a patronizing manner.[†]

If you're in the beauty business, recognize that customer preferences can vary considerably. One person may like to apply a dab of blush on the apple of their cheeks for a splash of color; while another may apply blush for super-bold contouring; and a third may carry the blush further up their cheekbones to create a youthful baby-doll look. Right now, both the 'Kylie

---

[*] https://www.cnbc.com/2019/08/12/versace-givenchy-and-coach-say-sorry-over-chinese-t-shirt-anger.html

[†] https://www.npr.org/sections/goatsandsoda/2018/12/01/671891818/dolce-gabbana-ad-with-chopsticks-provokes-public-outrage-in-china

Jenner' and the 'Kim K' styles are very popular, each with a high degree of contouring.

Digital Reviews

Digital reviews have greater potency and credibility in China than in most countries. You will want to monitor and respond to reviews in real time.

---

iPhone 12 reviews:

As a reminder that e-commerce in China has a stronger social element than other markets, compare 2020 reviews for iPhone 12 on different product pages around the world:

Tmall: 65,000 product reviews.
JD: 2,80,000 product reviews.
Amazon US: 24 reviews.
Amazon UK: 239 reviews.
Amazon Germany: 371 reviews.
Apple's home page: no reviews.*

The Chinese consumer likes authenticity and when they buy products, they want to know that the products are genuine, that they match their online descriptions, and that they live up to the overall quality expected from the brand. If they feel cheated or wronged, they don't just contact customer service to make their thoughts known. They post their thoughts in digital reviews so that the world knows.

Reviews and comments are found everywhere—from sites to platforms—and they can hurt a brand with their bluntness or help with

---

* https://appleinsider.com/articles/19/11/21/apple-pulls-all-customer-reviews-from-online-apple-store#:~:text=On%20November%2017%2C%20Apple%20removed,pages%20on%20the%20Apple%20website

their positivity. A brand must actively 'listen' to the consumers and monitor reviews.

This is such a significant phenomenon that it has given rise to a cottage industry in which reviews can be incentivized or paid. This is not a standard practice in other markets, but it illustrates that in China social reviews are an important marketing tool.

Rather than pay for reviews, we recommend a brand ensures that it does not leave its launch strategy to chance, that it has worked through a soft launch and focus groups to work out any potential problems in the product, the packaging, or the messaging. Then the brand can work with hired KOLs to launch on a positive footing.

Livestreaming

China is replete with livestreaming webcasts, much of it non-commercial, such as young people discussing their lives, offering diet tips, or demonstrating dance moves—similar to the role YouTube might play in other countries. But livestreaming has also become one of the most cost-effective tools for e-commerce in China, a bit like the home shopping TV shows in other markets, but with even greater variety and impact.

As an e-commerce tool, the typical livestreaming format involves a celebrity demonstrating a product and answering questions from a digital audience. It takes place in real-time and is usually followed on a smartphone. By 2020, the China live-streaming audience had passed 562 million, almost 60 per cent of all Internet users. Within that audience, some 309 million engaged in e-commerce, some 33 per cent of all Internet users,[*] generating projected sales of $148 billion, up 122 per cent from 2019.[†]

How big is livestreaming on holidays? According to Danielle Bailey, Senior Director, Global New Commerce, Nike,

During Singles' Day, brands are often livestreaming anywhere from 14 to 24 hours a day. We've even seen brands like L'Oréal experimenting

---

[*] China Internet report
[†] https://www.iimedia.cn/c400/75194.html

with the use of virtual avatars as hosts for livestreams in order to support them even during off hours.[*]

Or look at what JD did on 6.18 2020: Deborah Weinswig of Coresight Research noted that Xu Lei, CEO of JD Retail, together with actress Zheng Shuang, singer Da Zhangwei, and actor Guo Qilin

> .. . . raked in RMB 475 million [$69·9 million] in their six-hour long livestreaming show. They broke last year's 6·18 record by Top KOL Viya's of RMB 62 million [$9·1 million] per hour.[†]

Although there are multiple platforms and service providers, Alibaba's Taobao has the largest market share of livestreaming.

China Livestream Platform Overview

	Platform attribute	Major products	Modes of live commerce	Opportunity	GMV[‡]	Monthly active user[§] (MAUs)
Taobao Live	E-commerce	All categories in the Taobao ecosystem	Businesses live commerce and shopping assistants	Huge customer base and subordinate multi-channel company	500 billion	756 million

[*] https://alibaba.brand.live/c/11-11

[†] https://technode.com/2020/06/23/insider-e-commerce-is-back-and-big-on-6-18/

[‡] https://www-statista-com.libproxy1.nus.edu.sg/study/82597/live-commerce-in-china/ Statista: Livestreaming e-commerce in China

[§] https://www-statista-com.libproxy1.nus.edu.sg/study/82597/live-commerce-in-china/ Statista: Livestreaming e-commerce in China

Douyin	Content	Beauty makeup and clothes	Highly recommended, content, hot short video	Focus on innovative and novel content	200 billion	469 million
Kuaishou	Social + Content	Low price goods under100 RMB, like food, daily necessities, and clothing	Influencer livestream	Abundant KOL resources, cost-effective supply chain, low price-boost sales strategy	250 billion	470 million
JD.com	E-commerce	All categories selling in JD e-commerce ecosystem	Businesses live commerce and shopping guides	Huge customer base	Not available	268 million
Pinduoduo	E-commerce + Social	Agricultural products, small commodities, local specialties	Businesses live commerce	Group buy and low price	Not available	441 million

Why are consumers and brands both embracing this medium?

First, there's a functional advantage to livestreaming. It allows experts and peers to show the product being used, to talk through techniques and permutations, to demonstrate various techniques, and to point out the results. The audience can ask questions in anonymity, but the experience is interactive and immersive.

There's also a feeling of authenticity that comes from livestreaming. Remember, Chinese TV is entirely state-owned, with somewhat predictable plots and themes. And much of the advertising is scripted and airbrushed. Reviews and reactions of fellow consumers already weigh heavily on Chinese buyers' purchasing decisions, and livestreaming allows them to witness those reactions in real time. Okay, it is all a bit rehearsed and celebrities are not exactly everyday people, but nothing beats a live show for surprises and emotional impact. Livestreaming bridges the gap between advertising and a reality TV show.

Consumers feel vicariously that they are actually handling the product themselves. They're no longer picking a product off a shelf, they are now part of the process, shaping the outcome from the convenience of the living room sofa. The fact that it is real-time means the purchase can take place in real-time as well. The use of someone with public stature validates the results. The best livestreaming allows room for spontaneity, be it side chatter, a joke, or even a small mistake. After all, this is how friends talk with one another.

What is absent in livestreaming is the hard-sell shouting about the product that might occur in other settings. As consumers grow in sophistication and taste, they would rather participate in a conversation than be lectured to. Livestreaming invites the brand into the home in much the same way you would invite a friend. Hendrik Laubscher, CEO of Blue Cape Ventures explained to me,

> The entertainment and trust provided enables brands to lessen shopping cart abandonment, decrease returns and engage better with their consumers.

In this sense, livestreaming empowers the consumers. The brand must be responsive to viewers in real time because consumers have the power to hold them accountable through questions and probes. Livestreaming is closer to a job interview than to a product demo, with the audience conducting the interview. If it is a reality TV show, the consumer is the judge.

Most importantly, livestreaming allows brands to be introduced to consumers through a richer experience. Demonstrations allow for a dialogue that can cover more complex subject matter. In the beauty segment alone, there were over 19,000 livestreams on Taobao Live in the first half year of 2020 and these generated a GMV of 12 billion RMB, 20 per cent of the total Taobao Live GMV.[*]

---

[*] https://www.163.com/dy/article/FISNVSOB0531IJZM.html

Livestreaming can also be particularly potent for niche and new-to-market brands who do not have the ability to generate a buzz. Livestreaming provides assurance the product is used, accepted, and loved.

In that same vein, livestreaming can generate word of mouth. If you can explain it, you have internalized the brand's value proposition. Every product demo is like a wine tasting. Once the sommelier explains the wine to you, you can play that back in your head and repeat it to others. Now you have become the expert.

Ashley Dudarenok, Founder of ChoZan, explained to me the economics of livestreaming:

> The platform is getting the advertising dollars, the KOL is getting paid, the consumer is getting the promoted products at a competitive discount, but not for the brand. Brands are essentially paying for everything. They have to pay for advertising to boost the post on the platform, offer discounted products and invest money to build up these KOLs where they will need to pay again to access. This is precisely the reason why more and more brands are already beginning to nurture their own brand KOLs. Cooperating with brand KOLs can achieve a higher conversion rate and better support long term sales at a much lower cost.

Social Promotion

Social promotion drives brand awareness to a greater degree in China than in other markets. As Prof. Towson notes at the start of this chapter, this means that what your customers, fans, and followers think about you and say about you might have a greater impact in China than your paid advertising. So your communications strategy is to interact with customers, and to help them become proselytizers for your brand. Man-Chung Cheung of Insider Intelligence explained to me,

> Word-of-mouth is extremely important to Chinese consumers. They are known to be prolific users of social media for product research, looking for user feedback, and interacting with brands in all types of ways.

From playing games on Taobao and JD, to spinning a digital fortune wheel at a Tmall shop, to re-posting mini-apps on their WeChat feed, consumers in China enjoy interacting with platform promotions and sharing brand messaging, especially if there's a possibility of a giveaway, a group deal, a discount, or a coupon.

Mini-Apps

We mentioned mini-apps in our Chapter 9 discussion of platforms and social media. Think of mini-apps as mini-programs. They have several advantages over conventional apps and web pages. First, they are already integrated into the hosting platform such as WeChat for key functions such as search and payments. Second, they load instantly. Mini-apps are limited in size and because they are hosted on the major platforms, they require only one click to access. Third, web developers like them as well since the platform provides ready-made architecture.

Although first launched on WeChat, mini-apps operate on all major platforms such as Alipay and Meituan. Consumers can use mini-apps to make purchases, schedule appointments, or play games. Consumers use them to share photos, pay utility bills, hail taxis, get news, book doctors' appointments, and use government services. Tesla owners can locate charging stations.

Mini-apps provide a quick introduction to your brand and are particularly potent if you're offering a game or a time-saving feature. You can also sell through a mini-app. Mini-apps can list in-demand items that sell quickly through flash sales promotions. Mini-apps can also be used as a communications tool—brands can create interactive, visual features to engage customers and encourage them to share content with friends.

WeChat mini-apps support augmented reality (AR), which overlays virtual imagery on to the physical world. We provided the example in Chapter 5 how Armani's mini-app uses AR to allow users to test the look of various shades of lipstick through users' smartphone cameras.

Overview of leading mini-apps platforms

	Description	Traffic entrance	Active user[*]	Total number[†]	Example
WeChat	WeChat mini programs have different functions: food or groceries delivery, shopping, leisure and entertainment, life services, and ride hailing. Most programs are for life services such as social media, payments, and restaurant ordering.	Exploration tab, search engine, public account menu, public article page, QR code, wallet, contact card	DAU 400 million	3 million	Tesla created a mini program to help owners find charging stations, schedule a test-drive and share experiences. The shared-bike company, Mobike, built a mini-program to enable users to locate bikes, unlock bikes and top-up accounts.
Alipay	Alipay mini-apps also have different category functions: convenience services, shopping promotion and discount, transportation, life services and health services. It is designed to allow brands and services to provide richer O2O functionality.	Exploration tab, 'Kou bei'—a review sharing function, friend's list tab, public article page, QR code, wallet, status update page	MAU 600 million	2 million	Starbucks built an Alipay mini program to enable online ordering and on-demand delivery, a membership program, online gift cards and promotions

[*] http://www.cniteyes.com/index.php?app=widget&mod=ShowDocument&act=view&attach_id=7494&type=pdf
[†] Ibid.

| Baidu | Baidu uses mini-apps to direct content such as a 'popular list,' 'editor's collection', and 'recommended for you' | Personal center page, mini game, account menu | MAU 500 million | 4,20,000 | Little Red Book also joined Baidu mini-apps. A search for Xiaohongshu will show Xiaohongshu's mini-app on the first page. |

Brand Collaboration

The final element of marketing in China which is usually different than the home market approach is brand collaboration, by which we mean the cluster of tactics that give a brand greater potency such as co-branding, product-placement marketing, and brand-association marketing. Let's look at how cosmetics brands employ these three marketing tactics in China.

Co-branding

Co-branding allows established brands to get a lift from a new partner brand. Maybelline partnered with BigEve, a beauty brand founded by thirty-one-year-old Zhang Dayi, a KOL who also goes by the name BigEve Zhang. Their co-branded collection called BigEve × Maybelline contained lipsticks, 'gentle', 'little cute', 'cold little devil', and 'white red tomato'. BigEve's 11 million Weibo followers, mostly Gen Z, urban women from tier-two and -three cities, made the cooperation a good fit. The lipstick collection generated some $114,000 in sales in the first three months of its launch.

Beyond two-way unions, brands can also seek multi-party initiatives. Watsons, the largest beauty and personal care chain store in Asia, teamed with the '163 Music' app and reality show *Idol Producer* to launch six music-themed looks for brands featured in their China retail locations. These six makeup looks represented Jazz, Pop, Hip-Hop, Light Music, Ballad and Antique. Watsons invited boy bands from *Idol Producer* to perform, encouraged attendees to sing the songs from '163 Music', and offered makeup services to all. As a result, the Baidu search index for Watsons more than doubled throughout the event.

Product Placement Marketing

Product Placement marketing involves collaboration with original content such as movies, novels, or animation. From hashtags alone, this tends to generate the greatest digital buzz in the Chinese cosmetics market.

For example, L'Oréal Men launched a limited-edition product line when the movie *Avengers: Endgame* was shown in China. In addition to promotions on social media platforms such as Wechat, Weibo, LRB and Douyi, L'Oréal Men launched pop-up stores in major cinemas and advertised on digital ticketing channels. More than 1,00,000 units of limited-edition products were sold on Tmall during the movie's release.

Winona, a Chinese medical skincare brand, cooperated with Budding Pop, a cartoon meme popular among Chinese Gen Z and millennials, to launch a limited-edition collection of face masks during last year's Singles' Day. Different face masks featured one of four functions: anti-allergy, hydration, whitening and repair. Each mask came with tips on skin improvement. The face masks attracted approximately 30,000 buyers and generated $400,000 in sales during the one-day event. For the past twelve months, Winona has been one of the top ten beauty brands in sales on Tmall.

Other brands have not been slow to adapt to this marketing technique. Collaborating with the TV show *National Treasure*, L'Oréal launched a line of lipstick that evoked colors from ancient China, connecting both culture and history. Chando, the second best-selling Chinese beauty brand, cooperated with the video game 'Cross Fire', embedding its men's skincare line into the game by offering customized character's equipment and appearance.

Brand Association marketing

Brand Association marketing refers to branded collaboration with art and cultural events. Perfect Diary, a leading Chinese cosmetics brand, collaborated with the British Museum to launch two 'Fantastic' eye shadow kits. The eye shadow shades, one of warm colors and the other, cold, were inspired by Italian Renaissance 'maiolica' art. Both kits came with tote bags and a maiolica-shaped pair of earrings. Besides the glimmering, localized look of the kit, a large volume of branded articles and short videos posted by influencers helped drive sales and affinity. Education on maiolica art and Renaissance history were also provided on social media platforms, with content 'Provided by Perfect Diary'. This series of marketing tactics turned the kit into a top-ten product on Tmall. The collaboration generated $1·3 million during Singles' Day sales, bringing flagship store sales to almost $5 million.

Dermalogica Case Study

The Dermalogica case study illustrates that a range of marketing tactics should be used to enhance the overall effect of the marketing campaign. In this case, the brand is introducing not just a new product, but a new product category. Dermalogica is a California-based skin-care brand, owned by Unilever. They discovered that young Chinese women were interested in anti-aging products and hadn't yet been introduced to cream masks.

The company had entered the China market on Tmall Global, and started promoting its goods to financially independent women, aged 20–25, in major cities.

The company used Chinese celebrity marketing to their advantage, bringing in one celebrity for Little Red Book ads, a second for Sina Weibo ads, a third to stop by a shop, and a fourth to pose with the product. They also employed Key Opinion Leaders to market the product in a livestreaming event—selling thousands of masks in minutes.

Finally, they engaged in product promotion at shopping malls, exhibitions, and offline training sessions, along with product placements on TV shows and posts on Little Red Book, Sina Weibo, and WeChat.

Soon the item became the dominant product in mask sales on Tmall Global. The success of the mask opened the door to the company's many other successful products and storylines in China.

Their latest accomplishment? The company generated $26 million during 2020 Singles' Day extravaganza.

Key Takeaways

➢ Marketing and marketing communications are in many ways similar in China to what you find in your home market.

➢ But there are at least six clusters of differences, all of which have a digital dimension. The smart brands develop a program for each of these areas.

➢ Success in China depends on controlled experimentation and creativity in areas that might be different from your home market. Do not shy away from an initiative because you have never done it before.

13

Logistics and Finance

Every e-commerce strategy needs a finance strategy.

Since China e-commerce is the most advanced in the world, it should not be a surprise that the logistics and the finance mechanisms that support e-commerce are also perhaps the most advanced in the world. As with the recently discussed marketing strategies and platforms, taking advantage of the strengths of logistics and finance in China e-commerce can require some adjustment on behalf of the merchant—the more you can fit into their system, the more the system will work for you. Once a company is in the system, Chinese logistics and finance can provide better outcomes for both the merchant and the consumer. By 'logistics' I mean both legs, the international, in-bound leg of transportation as well as the domestic, last-mile leg. By 'finance' I also mean two legs: how the merchant finances the inventory (trade finance) and how the consumer finances the purchase.

We will discuss all four elements below.

But let me begin with two e-commerce stories, one from a consumer perspective and one from a merchant perspective, that have happy endings provided by logistics and finance mechanisms.

The first story: You are having lunch with your office friends in Shanghai, just a bunch of guys relaxing a bit at mid-day—and you are struck with an uncomfortable thought. It is your wife's birthday today and you have not selected a present. What to do?

You immediately crowd-source some ideas from your lunch buddies: What did you get your wife for her last birthday? What was the nicest gift you got your wife in the past year? Or you can use Baidu to search online and ask, as you would in any country: 'Best gift for wife's birthday.'

The happy ending: You can order the gift on your smartphone from the lunch table at noon and it will be delivered by 5 p.m. Relationship saved—by e-commerce and by logistics.

Another story: You are a German merchant running a mid-tier family business, a *mittelstand*. You are a leading brand in your segment of consumer electronics and you opened up an e-commerce store in China eighteen months ago. In those eighteen months, sales have gone from a €1 mil run-rate to €5 mil.

You cannot tie up €5 mil to finance inventory because you are also pursuing growth in the EU and other markets. You need financial support.

The happy ending: Ant Financial or Cainao, both Alibaba-linked companies, provide loans based on inventory that allow you to finance your rapid growth. You can essentially get trade finance in China without ever submitting financial statements or going through a formal credit evaluation. The fact that you are selling through Tmall provides a commercial history to the lender, and the fact that you are using the Cainao warehouse systems means Cainao can offer a loan against the goods.

So, in China, logistics and finance are force-multipliers for e-commerce, not just ancillary activities.

Logistics

As with marketing, after all is said and done, much of what you do in logistics might be an enhanced version of what you are doing in your home market. You might even use the same freight forwarder or express company. It would not hurt to start the conversation with a call to UPS, Fedex, DHL, or whomever you currently use. Or you could attend a webinar one of those groups might produce. There are strong China-based companies such as SF Express that have good global reach, and there are China-oriented logistics companies such as FlexPort that will customize a China solution for you.

Alibaba and JD offer logistics solutions as well. As mentioned above, Cainao is the Alibaba subsidiary that runs a global logistics service inbound to China, along with integrated warehouses.

This is a particularly appealing solution for companies that are using the cross-border model, such as Tmall Global or JD Worldwide as discussed in Chapter 9. You can fill Chinese consumer orders at your home fulfilment center where you fulfil your domestic e-commerce orders. The order is filled, packed, and ready to go at the warehouse dock and Cainao or JD will get your package to China. From a brand's perspective, that's good news. Customers are receiving better cargo rates due to sheer volume pricing and your goods can arrive to the Chinese customer in three to five days. Most important, the cross-border model means your company does not have to establish an overseas inventory pool, so China launch costs are kept low.

As your brand matures in the market, you can keep the cross-border model but establish a separate fulfilment center in the region, such as in Hong Kong or in the Shanghai Free Trade Zone (FTZ). An FTZ means that there are no testing or labelling requirements, that VAT is paid only after the goods are sold, and that the products can be used in other markets if necessary. Fulfilling orders out of Hong Kong or an FTZ maintains the legal requirement of an off-shore sale, but moving that fulfilment to an adjacent locale shaves time and money from logistics. Think about doing this once your sales reach, say, $1–2 million a year.

An ongoing theme of this book is that the complexity of your solution should not exceed the value of the project; in other words, to ensure that costs and benefits are lined up. So, you might want to start with the cross-border model fulfilled from your domestic operations, migrate to a China-proximate fulfilment center when your sales reach $1–2 million a year, and migrate to an in-country model once your sales reach $5 million. The in-country model will require up-front investments but will result in lower unit logistics, lower costs to consumers, faster delivery time, and greater reach within China.

In other words, your in-bound logistics strategy has as much to do with you and your China strategy as it does with China. If you have a strong shipping department already, well-versed in international solutions, blending China into the mix should be relatively easy. Similarly, if you are large enough to invest in China you might want to start day one with an in-country solution. But if you are a smaller firm, you might not have much of a shipping department to begin with, you might have a more limited budget, and you might not have much in the way of familiarity with international markets. In this latter instance, the cross-border solution is probably a better fit.

The International Model

Whether you migrate to an in-country model or to a cross-border model with China-adjacent fulfilment, you will want to move to ocean shipping as quickly as you can. As illustrated below, the cost savings for ocean shipping are considerable and typically outweigh the costs of a slower delivery cycle.

As with shipping anywhere, that cost depends on weight, size, distance, volume, and relationship with your current logistics provider, your freight forwarder, or your e-commerce platform. Major service providers such as Cainao and JD can handle shipping as well as air freight.

But here's one example: if you had to air freight 500 lbs from Miami to Shanghai, a breakdown could look something like this. Note that in this example the goods are trucked to Chicago to get the best air freight pricing:

- Airfreight: $1.90/kg (VIA China Southern Airlines): $431
- Airport Transfer: $0.15/kg (min $35): $35
- Handling: $65
- Automated Export System (AES): $35
- Documentation Fee: $45
- Trucking fee from Miami to Chicago: $430

The total cost for a Miami-Shanghai air freight shipment would be **$1041**

However, if you were able to use sea shipment instead, a breakdown would look like this. In this example, Savannah is used because the freight forwarder has identified available capacity. Although the trucking costs to Savannah is $300, trucking the goods from a Miami warehouse to the Port of Miami would still cost $100.

- Sea freight: $1.00/kg or $225
- Trucking fee from Miami to Savannah: $300
- Documentation: $110

The total cost of sea freight for a 500 lbs cargo would be around **$635** and the shipment would take 44–48 days. Of course, this cost differential must be considered in the context or your business model, value chain strategy, and customer requirements.

The Last Mile

Chinese consumers have higher expectations than most western consumers, and the logistics system understands those expectations are a key part of customer satisfaction.

In the United States, people think two-day shipping is impressive. Americans pay their $100 yearly fee for Amazon Prime and they're content.

In major Chinese cities such as Shanghai or Guangzhou, residents expect same-day delivery or even half-day delivery, without any annual fee. And Cainao's goal is to be able to offer twenty-four-hour delivery anywhere in China for about 30 cents.[*]

This is not only a powerful boon to the consumer, it helps the merchant as well. If every item can be delivered the same day, every purchase can be an impulse purchase. Why take even twenty minutes to go to the local store, when the e-commerce product will be delivered in a few hours?

The U-Turn Model

As a foreign company, can you start selling products in China if you already make your products in a Chinese factory?

Just because a product is manufactured in China does not mean it is approved to be sold in China. Indeed, some of the contract

---

[*] https://time.com/5914173/cainiao-logisitics-alibaba-china-trade/

manufacturing that takes place in China takes place in specially designated export processing zones which require all products to be exported out of China. Additionally, being manufactured in China does not automatically mean that the product will be approved by the Chinese regulatory body.

But, as with most challenges in China, there are also solutions. The most common is called the U-Turn Model in which your Chinese factory ships your goods offshore and then you hire a freight forwarder—be it Cainao or someone else—to send products back to China. Sometimes this is done through physical transfer, the product has to be moved in and out of China, but increasingly we are seeing this solved through the payment of a fee. In other words, the merchant would have to pay a rebate to the export-processing zone for any goods that were not being exported.

Finance

As mentioned earlier, finance means both helping the merchant finance inventory and helping the Chinese consumer finance purchases.

Finance Strategy: Merchant

An e-commerce strategy needs a finance strategy, or at least financial awareness and planning. The main reason is that as sales start to grow in e-commerce channels, the cash cycle can start to deteriorate.

A typical wholesale model might be based on 30- or 60-day payment terms. But a China e-commerce model can add complexity to this for several reasons:

—Shipping and time to market can add several weeks to the supply chain;
—Payment from the platform can add two more weeks. On platform sales, funds from consumers are held in escrow for two weeks to ensure goods reach the customer in good order;

—The nature of e-commerce reduces predictability. You might launch a new product line hoping to reach $1 million in sales on 6.18, but the new line only reaches $800 thousand in sales. Not bad, perhaps from a marketing point of view, but the finance people are wondering when the missing $200 thousand will show up.

There are a range of solutions to these new challenges. Companies can finance this change in the cash cycle out of pocket. Alternatively, a distributor can absorb some of this cost and volatility, but the merchant gives up some margin. Finally, a merchant can arrange financial support from outside parties such as a commercial bank or Cainao, as the German mittelstand company did in the story at the start of this chapter.

Finance Strategy: Consumer

China is perhaps the most cash-free society in the world, with electronic payment systems widely integrated into the smartphone culture. But credit cards are not the answer in China e-commerce. China shoppers use Alipay to purchase items on Taobao, Tmall, and Tmall Global and they use WeChatPay to purchase items on WeChat or JD. Alipay and WeChatPay are debit mechanisms which execute payment through the consumer's bank account or credit cards. Through Alipay, consumers can also be offered an instalment pay option, Huabei.

Huabei enables consumers to pay for online and offline purchases within a monthly credit limit set by Alipay. For example, if a consumer wishes to purchase an item over three months, the interest is 1.8 per cent interest, and if over 6 months, the interest is 4.5 per cent. As with credit around the world, the credit limits can be increased over time. The merchant can decide whether to absorb the Huabei costs or to allow the consumer to pay the interest, adding flexibility to sales as well.

Payment and Remittance

From the merchant perspective, payments and remittances are relatively straightforward.

The merchant takes no payment risk on the platforms because the customer must pay in full at the time of purchase. If the customer is using Huabei or a credit card, the full purchase amount is still credited to the merchant at time of purchase.

If the merchant is using a cross-border model, the goods will be paid to you off-shore in the currency of your choice, be it US dollars, Euros, or Australian dollars.

If you are using the in-country model, you are formally importing the goods and selling them in China for RMB, which then has to be converted to your currency and remitted. This is not a complicated process, but you need to ensure all of your goods were legally imported through proper channels and you have the appropriate documentation.

In short, payment and remittances from China are a regularized, everyday occurrence. You need to make sure your paperwork is in order but remitting funds from China is largely the same as remitting them from any other major market.

Key Takeaways

➤ Logistics and finance can both be big boosts to your China e-commerce efforts, but you will need to adjust to fit into existing systems.

➤ Calibrate your activity commensurate with your sales. You do not have to start with the most comprehensive solution on day one.

➤ Time is never your friend. Especially if you are new to market, you will need to budget extra time for multiple approval processes and paperwork.

14

How to Fail in China

The most common causes of failure in China are because of the company, not because of China.

May we discuss car accidents? Every accident has a different cause, but if we were to look at a number of them, patterns would emerge and we could group the causes into general categories: those caused by driver error; those due to the behavior of another car; those due the weather, or due to mechanical failure.

This analogy came to me when I served as Undersecretary for International Trade in the US Department of Commerce. Among my responsibilities was export promotion for the entire US Government, so we ran a range of outreach activities, workshops, presentations, trade missions, as well as sectoral programs and one-on-one problem-solving and counselling.

Over the course of three years, I connected with some 2000 companies on the topic of how to take their companies to new markets. At Export Now, we have met with or presented to several thousand more companies on China strategy. The result of all this is several thousand lessons in what to do and what not to do.

You will be glad to know that there were not many car crashes in these groups, but one of the surprise findings was the lack of correlation between a company's success in its home market and its success overseas, a pattern I see every day in China. In other words, you might be a very safe driver back home but that does not mean you won't encounter problems in China.

This disconnect between home market success and China failure suggests there are a set of skills or management disciplines that are unrelated to home market success but necessary for China success.

I will try to walk through these skills and disciplines in this chapter. First, I will share the two most common causes of failure, then we will look at a few case studies, and finally we will draw some general conclusions.

The Two Most Common Reasons Companies Fail: Goals and Plans

The most common cause of failure is the lack of an internal consensus on goals at the company. Are you going to China in search of greater sales or profits, or a desire to maintain segment leadership, or a defensive move as your competitors become more international, or an efficiency move as international sales allow you to scale, or as a diversification tactic so you are not over-reliant on one market?

Most brands have an assortment of goals, with the first mentioned— greater sales or profits—usually leading the list. Your company needs to make sure an internal consensus has been reached that will support your China strategy. And that is usually not a stand-alone China strategy, but the China element of your international strategy.

A failure to agree on goals is bad enough, but it spills over into **the second most common cause of failure: No plan.** These two areas of failure are definitely related in that if you have no certainty of goals, it is difficult to establish your budget and your timetable. And related to budget and timetable, what are your success metrics? Do you need to hit break-even in one year? Will you quit the market if you are at 80 per cent of break-even? What if you are at 50 per cent of break-even, but growing 50 per cent annually?

A plan should involve more than a discussion. The company needs to conduct a market study and competitive research. There needs to be an internal discussion on China strategy and what might work. Why not discuss your competitors' advertising and social media? You do not want your company to buy into the *Law of Convergence*—but not read the other chapters of the book.

Instead, there are several additional steps you can take:

—Have a formal market research study done. A 'quick and dirty' research project might cost something like $10,000.

—Purchase competitors' products from their China website. You can evaluate the product, the packaging, and the customer service.

—Cultivate partners and friends in the market. Use them as your focus group.

And smarter companies know that success metrics in China—as in most new markets—are unlikely to be the same as the home market.

In sum, **the most common causes of failure in China is because of the company, not because of China.**

Lessons from Case Studies

Let's see what we can learn from four car crashes.

Case Study: IKEA—A Differing Standard

The Swedish home furnishing giant IKEA suffered more than a black eye in China a few years ago with its clumsy handling of a product recall. All, unfortunately, a result of its own bad decisions.

In 2016, IKEA announced it would recall almost 1·7 million chests and dressers in China. The issue was whether the drawers could pose a danger to children if the furniture was not properly fixed to walls, said China's leading consumer safety agency, the General Administration of Quality Supervision, Inspection and Quarantine.

The announcement represented a reversal of IKEA's statement from just a week before when IKEA stated it would not extend a recall of 36 million dressers in North America to China after the products were linked to six child deaths.

So, one safety standard for the West, and another one for China? Ouch. This led the official Xinhua news agency to criticize IKEA for showing 'arrogance'. IKEA started to fix the problem, but the damage to its reputation had been done.

Lessons for your brand:

1. **One Global Standard.** Tastes and purchasing power can differ around the world. But when it comes to matters of ethics, such as health and safety, your company should enforce the same standard in every market.
2. **A legal defense is not a reputational defense.** IKEA was technically not out of compliance with Chinese safety requirements as they are different from US requirements. But this defense falls flat in the court of public opinion. IKEA was essentially implying it will only follow a minimal approach to safety.
3. **It was not over quickly.** Even under criticism, IKEA was still reacting to the story and not working to resolve the reputational damage. It needed to think through a broader response. If Xinhua says you have a problem, you have a problem.

Case study: Apple—The Blame Game

This is not a car crash *per se*, but a look at how an iconic brand can fade in appeal. In 2019, Apple roiled the markets when CEO Tim Cook caught many by surprise and reduced the company's revenue forecast. He attributed the drop to slower economic growth in China, which prompted a bevy of news stories on the country's slowing economy. But, put me down as a sceptic, China's economic growth rate might not be a major factor here, if at all.

Lessons for your brand:

1. **Be careful of exculpatory statements.** When a CEO proclaims that results will be off solely because of factors outside of his control, this is usually a giveaway. Of course, no company is perfect, and no CEO is perfect. But Cook is essentially saying, 'This is not my fault. It's not me, it's you'—'you' being China. The problem with this explanation is that China has become more prosperous and tech-oriented since Apple entered the market, making it a more promising market for the tech giant from Cupertino. Apple has simply been unable to fully capture the market's potential.

2. **Apple might be good at tech and not good at competition.** Steve Jobs's view was that if your product was sufficiently advanced and if your brand were sufficiently cool, there would be no such thing as competition. Indeed, in many markets in which Apple operates, it has no direct competition. It is its own category of devices and gadgets. The consumer goes there because there are no viable alternatives. There is no competition from France, the UK or Germany, for example, not Nokia nor Blackberry. Sure, Samsung and the broader field of Androids are competitors, but Apple's dominance resembles that of IBM in the personal computer market back in the 1980s: there is no other game in town.

In China, however, there are brands that can go head-to-head with Apple, both in terms of technology and the buzz factor. Nobody was cooler than Steve Jobs at a new product launch, with the stage all to himself and attired simply in a black turtleneck. But that doesn't mean other brands can't do the same. Sure enough, Xiaomi CEO Lei Jun started doing new product launches with the stage all to himself and attired in a black turtleneck. If this stage presence defines your brand, it might be time to refresh.

3. **Is the 'replacement' marketing model still valid?** Every Apple consumer probably doesn't need a replacement phone every time a new model is introduced. China has a strong tech culture, a strong youth culture, a strong consumer culture, and a strong novelty culture. And the Apple iPhone sat right in the middle of this four-element Venn diagram. But what happens when Apple's mystique begins to fade in the eyes of consumers? China's youth culture is still present for now, but demographics show that the society is aging. Being the hippest person in the room is no longer as important as it once was. Consumer culture is still important, but saving money has its merits, too. Consumers don't need new iPhones, but they may very well want them, which are two very different matters.

4. **Where is Apple's Mercedes 190?** In other words, what is Apple's defensive strategy? Apple does not have a 'fighter brand', with a lower

price offering.* There are plenty of strategic markets in the world, and there are plenty of less-affluent markets. But China is the only market that is both strategic and not yet wealthy. Apple was used to competing in the other developed markets, primarily Europe and Japan, and never developed a special product or brand or pricing strategy for China. We can treat China the way we treat wealthy markets. The trouble with this strategy is that it fails to account for the bulk of the consumer market, the aspirational middle-class that would love to own an iPhone, but can't afford to buy one. So, in walks the local competition.

No need to spend $1200 on an iPhone when you can spend $800 on a Huawei or a Pixel, and you can spend the money that was saved on a new pair of Nikes and still have money left over. Mercedes has a powerful brand and, in many respects, it dominates its category. But when BMW and Audi started creeping up the value chain, Mercedes realized it needed to be able to speak to a different segment of consumers so, in 1982, they brought out the first compact Mercedes-Benz, the 190. Did Apple successfully develop a less expensive product for China or did it simply cede the bulk of the market to local competitors? Chinese alternatives to Apple, like Huawei, Oppo, Vivo, TCL, ZTE, and Lenovo offer consumers significant value in China and now in other global markets.

To be fair to Cook, China's growth is indeed slowing though it remains in positive territory. But Apple's problem in China is not China, it's Apple.

Case Study: Janey James Soap

Janey James Soap manufactures an organic all-in-one liquid cleanser for women that could be used for hand washing, face washing and even clothes washing.

Lessons for your brand:

---

* 'Should you launch a fighter brand?' https://hbr.org/2009/10/should-you-launch-a-fighter-brand

1. **Market segmentation**: The Chinese female consumer, like many around the planet, typically prefers different soaps for different purposes. This alone reduces the appeal of an all-in-one soap.
2. **Price and quality still matter**: Beyond the confusing brand position, Janey James was also priced above market, and there was an important quality problem: the soap tended to dry out the user's hair and face. These three problems meant that the product was a challenging sell in the market.
3. **Organic varies in appeal**: One of the products' strengths meant less in China: the appeal of organic products is growing more slowly in China than in the United States.

The company could have positioned the product, targeting only one market segment such as hand washing. Or it could have lowered the price and positioned it as a body wash. But either choice would have been a bit different from its home market position, and the company was unwilling to adjust. As a result, it continues to lag in the market.

Case Study: Simply Real—The Lack of Narrative

Simply Real (SR) had a lot going for it. The product was simple enough—a foam cosmetic applicator—but that simplicity meant low costs as well, and repeat purchases. SR entered the China market in 2015 and by 2019 had gone up 100x in sales, from $200k to $20 million in annual sales, and did so with modest digital advertising and by selling mainly on one platform, Tmall Global.

But in 2019, there were several shifts. SR was sold to a US private equity firm with a keen eye on operations and with no particular China-marketing background. Their specialty was sourcing, and cost-control. Second, a Chinese brand, Perfect Diary, entered the market and in 2019 alone went from 3 per cent to 15 per cent market share.

SR was not looking at China growth or China strategy, it was looking at how to cut costs. China e-commerce was growing 20–30 per cent a year. SR, as market leader, was growing over 100 per cent a year. China retail strategy dictates that initially brand strategy should be oriented by scale: grow big fast. As brands mature, they should shift their priority to net profit, by improving sourcing, logistics, operations, and even by negotiating improved terms with their service providers. But this change in focus would be more important to SR as the brand hits $50 mil in sales, less important when the brand was at $10 mil.

Lessons for your brand:

1. **Don't take your foot off the gas pedal.** SR decided to reduce its new product launch cycle and cancel social media. This saves money in the short run, but it allows competitors to gain market share. Also, there is a second-order effect. Others in the e-commerce ecosystem, such as Alibaba, see that you are taking your foot off the gas pedal. Others are less likely to believe in you if you do not believe in yourself.

2. **Play to your strength.** SR had core strengths in China, notably being the established market leader. The best way to maintain this leadership position would be to pursue every distribution channel possible and build that leadership into ubiquity. Yet SR decided not to go ahead with distribution through one of the larger convenience store chains in China because they stated there was not enough margin in the deal for them. SR also cancelled long-established plans to migrate from Tmall Global to Tmall.com.

Both of these decisions were mistakes. Getting national distribution even without a big net would have protected SR's position as segment leader and precluded the distributor from stocking competing brands. A defensive strategy might matter as much as offensive strategy. Additionally, SR would be in a stronger position to negotiate with other chains.

Not going on Tmall.com might have been a bigger mistake as much of the work to migrate had been done. It took SR two years to decide to open up a Tmall store. In China, things happen on a much more rapid timeframe. SR allowed the Tmall relationship to deteriorate by pushing back the Tmall.com strategy, cutting social media and cutting new product launches.

3. **You need a brand narrative.** The SR product is relatively low-tech. The market offers low barriers to entry. The product develops a cachet when it is endowed with premium attributes. But SR had a

premium position because it was new to the market and it enjoyed nice growth over four years. It never believed it had to invest in the brand. Meanwhile, Perfect Diary was hustling. Without a narrative and a strategy, a brand is just a label.

Conclusions:

What do we learn from IKEA, Apple, Janey James, and Simply Real? Each brand has a different set of problems, but we can add the following to the two common areas of failure—absence of goals and plans—discussed at the start of this chapter:

1. **Time Horizon**: Businesses with unrealistic expectations, looking for large gains in a short period of time. These same businesses don't understand that even though they are a market leader elsewhere, they are new to market in China. A business ignores its multi-year plan, packs it up, and leaves China before it pays any dividends. Draw up a different timeline for success. Think in a three-year term.

2. **Autopilot**: Businesses not being flexible in product development or differentiation. They underestimate the local competition and innovation taking place. This is the failure embodied in the *More of the Same* strategy discussed in Chapter 4.

3. **Retail skills**: These are companies that don't know how to sell directly to Chinese consumers. Historically, they have sold to retailers and not engaged directly with the end consumer. These companies must learn how to win the heart, soul, and trust of that customer. Whether it's dealing with someone posting a negative review or being outbid on a search keyword, you must roll up your sleeves and get in there. It's time for hand-to-hand combat.

4. **The lack of agility**: Businesses not fully understanding how fast China rolls out new channels, programs, initiatives. Not moving forward at 'China Speed'. If your company has always held to an annual roll-out of new products, but your main competitor in China has a quarterly roll-out, it might be time for a rethink.

5. **Bad fit**: Businesses not entering with a strong differentiator, a strong brand story or any brand awareness. Sometimes there is just too much

competition already. These businesses have little to no momentum. They're pretty much stuck in the mud. Unless these businesses are willing to spend tons and tons of money to build awareness and create a China brand story, their success is going to be minimal.

Not every company belongs in China. You need to have the wherewithal to succeed, and your business model has to be able to make the leap to the China operating environment. Fortunately, e-commerce helps you make the leap at a minimal cost.

No one is destined to fail in China. Normally, failure comes from a set of behaviors within the company. It's not that China is doing something wrong.

Key Takeaways

➤ Failures in China come from many different root causes, but they tend to fall into several groups. The most common reasons for failure is the inability to agree on a China goal and adopt a China plan.

➤ Beyond that, the failure to adapt or modify the business strategy is a leading cause of failure.

➤ Failure in China generally stems from mistakes made by the company, not challenges in the market.

15

How to Win in China

Time To Get Started

*If you want to see the future, look at China**

Mark Schneider, CEO Nestlé

What have we learned in this book so far? No one can claim there is only one route to succeed in China. There are many paths to making an entry and winning in the market. But we also know there are certain approaches that greatly enhance the likelihood of winning.

In this chapter we summarize those approaches and offer a three-year illustrative budget. Then we discuss steps you can take right away to start the journey.

The core takeaway on winning in China: You need to manage both the upside and the downside. There is enormous opportunity to win in this market and there are also costs and risks. Let's talk about both:

Manage the upside

E-commerce, over the long run, is an upside model because it allows you to scale with growing efficiency. It does not take ten times the work of a

---

* https://www.economist.com/business/2021/01/02/the-next-big-thing-in-retail-comes-with-chinese-characteristics

$1 million store to run a $10 million store. You will always want to invest in your brand, in the platforms, and in new products, but this can be done on a step-by-step basis.

However, victory needs to be earned. There needs to be something special in your product, your brand, or your digital message that allows the Chinese consumer to fall in love with you. This might require experimentation, and this might be a journey before you get it right.

You will likely need an approach that is not identical to your home market approach. You probably want to start small, using a cross-border model on one platform.

Partnerships, friends on the ground, research, analytics, are all part of the process. This facilitates transparency, accountability, feedback, and adaptation. This has been built into your home market over the years, perhaps without your being fully aware of it. Now you need to construct it anew in China without having to immediately or completely construct a parallel team.

You need to figure out a way to get started, to get a management consensus on a multi-year plan, and to help educate your leadership. This chapter will tackle these issues and more on getting started below.

Manage the downside

Simultaneous with managing the upside of China, you need to manage the potential costs and risks. E-commerce greatly reduces those costs and risks, but it does not eliminate them. It does not take bad management or a bad product and make them good. But if it reduces costs by 90 per cent then it reduces the break-even point by 90 per cent. E-commerce also provides rapid feedback, transparency, and real-time testing—all strong risk-management tools. And there are other steps you can take to manage the downside.

Avoid debt and exposure: The best approach for most international brands is the 'trading company' model in which you are simply selling products into the market and taking revenue back home. In this respect, e-commerce is your best friend. You can reach 900 million Chinese consumers through the e-commerce giants, and you do not need a China office or any personnel in country to do so.

Work with trusted partners: Do not rely solely on an array of local partners to solve China problems. Your auditors, your bank, and your law firm will have China branches or affiliates. Spend some time with them. Use a US third-party agency (TP)—such as, as you know by now, the one I work for—with your e-commerce channels.

Heavy up on communication and outreach: Your website should have a Chinese-language version. Your leadership should visit China at least once a year. Upgrade your knowledge with Alibaba and JD webinars. As an aside, the more you invest and learn, the more you may develop a passion for China. It's not required, but you wouldn't be the first person to begin liking China, its people, and its culture. By welcoming the journey, it's no longer just a job, there can be a joyous, unexpected payoff, as well.

Move incrementally: Even if you could reach $5 million in sales in your first year, why not adjust that to a target of $3 million? You can always build on these numbers as your comfort grows. **Experiment, adjust, get feedback.**

Your P&L Statement

Every business needs a Profit and Loss (P&L) statement which provides a road map of revenue and expenses and allows you to plan. What would a reasonable P&L look like for a company that was brand new to market? Some companies want to jump in with both feet and have the resources to make an all-in commitment. However, we more frequently see companies with more of a testing approach. For example, for a consumer goods company, I advise building a business plan around a first-year target of $1 million as a reasonable starting point and this allows you to experiment and refine over the course of that first year. Here's how that $1 million starting point might look.

Marketing Fees—20 to 40 per cent of annual sales should be devoted to marketing, depending on brand presence. You may not need that much if you're a popular brand or if you already have some presence in the market. On the other hand, you may want to spend more if you're new to the scene and aiming for exceptional growth. Marketing will typically be your single greatest expense. Included in the marketing budget is a 5 per cent set-aside of annual sales for the gifting of free products, a common element of promotions in China.

Platform Hosting Fees—Tmall and JD will charge roughly 5 per cent of annual sales to host a store on their platform. This also includes Alipay fees.

Logistics and Distribution Fees—15 to 20 per cent of annual sales for logistics, shipping, returns and exchanges, assuming this is cross-border.

Agency Fees—10 to 15 percent of annual sales. This is the fee for your China agent to work with you on strategy and goals, run your e-commerce store, manage financial settlement, and provide reports and analytics.

	YEAR ONE	YEAR TWO	YEAR THREE
SALES REVENUE	$1 Mil	$2 Mil	$4 Mil
EXPENSES			
Marketing	$200K to $400K	$400K to $700K	$800K to $1·2M
Commissions	$50K	$100K	$200K
Logistics	$150K to $200K	$300K to $350K	$550K to $650K
Agency Fees	$100K to $150K	$200K to $300K	$400K to $600K
Cost of Goods Sold	$300K	$600K	$1·2M
Total Costs	**$800K to $1·1M**	**$1·6M to $2·05M**	**$3·15M to $3·85M**
EBITDA	$200K to $100K	$400K to $50K	$850K to $150K

The above table is illustrative, and your results are likely to differ, but it is consistent with what I have seen working in China e-commerce. And note that this table does not include one-off costs such as web site design, platform registration fees, and possible management trips to China.

How many friends do you want in China?

When I worked in banking in China, I had one iron-clad rule for clients who were doing business there: your CFO should either be a foreign national or based offshore. Why? Because you need to have a CFO you can find and pursue legal action against if it comes to that.

That might sound a bit draconian, but it's a fact of life that companies conducting e-commerce overseas do not enjoy the same safeguards and legal protections they have in their home markets, and China is no different. While most Chinese partners are law-abiding, without the threat of legal sanctions as a deterrent, the possibility of malfeasance increases.

Yet, when I look today at international companies that are involved in China e-commerce, I find that many have entered the market fixed on one goal—delivering goods to customers at the lowest possible cost. Many rely heavily on outsourcing their operations to a local third-party e-commerce provider. As a result, they lack a fundamental element of accountability in the management of their mainland operations, as well as the breadth of management talent and problem-solving expertise that can help them deal with the range of challenges that may arise.

Can a company manage a cost-effective China e-commerce program from overseas, without an extensive and costly management team on the ground? The answer is yes, but companies need to be creative in how they tap local expertise. Part of the solution is to cultivate and involve more 'friends' than you normally might in your home market, making 'soft management' rather than hardcore legal deterrence a tool when working with local companies.

One example: involve the China branch of your home bank in your e-commerce operation. In your home market, you might meet with your banker a few times a year. In China, I suggest you meet with them every time you visit China. Local bankers can offer valuable insights to help monitor your on-the-ground business. What do they see when they look at your account? Any warning signs? What type of fraudulent activity is the most common in China? What are the indicators of fake sales or collusions in purchasing? Any extra safeguards necessary?

Similarly, you can undertake discussions with the China branch of your accounting firm to ensure you remain compliant with international audit standards and your inventory control is up to par. You should also meet with your law firm's China office to ensure you are compliant with the Foreign Corrupt Practices Act and that mechanisms are in place to avoid kickbacks. Meet with your ad agency to see if the click-through rates look genuine.

Beyond your immediate circle of professional services, why not engage an e-commerce firm for special assignments? You can work with this firm to establish a secret shopper program to monitor your order fulfilment and customer service activity. Or why not have this firm undertake a competitive analysis to understand what your competitors are doing? Or they could study competitive social media programs. Or review social media comments. Any of these steps would give you a little more control and insight.

Improving the breadth and frequency of discussions with your partners puts extra sets of eyes on your business to guard against undesired results, whether they be weak performance or actual malfeasance. Your bank helps manage your local finance director. Your accounting firm helps manage inventory. Your local e-commerce service provider should be able to answer questions from your CFO, your general counsel, and others in your organization.

In other words, the best China solution is rarely an all-China solution. Be a friendly sceptic and enlist help from international-standard firms for the perspective and expertise they offer. How many friends do you want in China? As many as you can get.

How to Get Started

British novelist L.P. Hartley once wrote,

> The past is another country. They do things differently there.[*]

China reminds us that the future is also another country, and things will be done differently there.

What we can say about consumers in this future is that they embrace technology, they love e-commerce, and they aren't afraid to make a purchase. Chinese customers are spending billions of dollars online as they search platforms for premium brands and become further captivated by holiday promotions, novel products, and technological innovations. This is great news for the nimble and the creative; bad news for the slow moving or the unimaginative.

The paradox of China market entry is that on any given day, it is a bad idea. It takes too much time. There are start-up costs. It can be unpleasant getting outside your comfort zone. It is never the right day to go to China.

But cumulatively, it is a good idea. Once you start to take the journey, the journey makes sense. Not only does it make sense, but you feel good about it. It is always the right time to go to China.

In other words, the best time to start was yesterday. The second-best time is today.

Let's say you are ready. How do you really start the process? What's the first move to make? Here are your first steps:

- Start doing your homework. Begin researching your market segment in China and what your competitors are doing. You can hire a China research firm to do this—heck, I'll do it for you—or you can hire a business student from a local college;
- Talk with your current service partners for guidance and advice, including your bank and your logistics firm;
- Attend webinars or programs of your country's leading China business and international trade organizations such as the US–China Business

---

[*] Hartley, L.P., *The Go-Between*.

Council or the British Chamber of Commerce. Similarly, you can go on a trade mission to China and connect with your country's export promotion agency.

- Reach out to China e-commerce platforms and China digital solution companies, for their thoughts. Alibaba and JD run webinars around the world to answer questions and explain their offerings;
- Start an internal planning process. How much of an investment are you prepared to make and over what time period?
- Ask your legal advisor to start the registration process in China for your name and trademarks, a step that should be taken whether a China move is immediate or not.

Finally, let's modify the fable of 'The Tortoise and the Hare'. Slow and steady won't win the race. Yes, you need patience, wisdom and determination. But you need to know when to listen, reorientate, and accelerate, as well. In China, it's fast and steady. You need to be both the tortoise and the hare.

The discussion about China e-commerce success is never-ending. There are always new players and new tactics. But we hope this book has helped you and your company understand the landscape and decide to make the China step.

We'll now step aside.

You have customers waiting.

Key Takeaways

- ➤ You should manage both the upside and the downside of China e-commerce.
- ➤ A three-year time horizon is a useful tool.
- ➤ Start researching, start planning, start making something happen.

16

From China to the World

We're going to have a record year as a company worldwide. We will also have a record year as a company within China. We've been growing within China at very high double-digit growth for a number of years now. That trend will continue this year. And online sales in general and really Tmall in particular will continue to grow as a percentage of the total business. So we're thrilled with the success of our business worldwide and particularly thrilled with the success of our business in China.[*]

—Andy Mooney, CEO, Fender Guitars

Engaging with the Chinese consumer is not only about 'making money', but is also about being at the cutting edge of knowledge and inspirations borne out from the innovations. And, the latter will be core to the long-term capability building for any company.

—comment from Edward Tse,
Founder and CEO, Gao Feng Advisory

How many thousands of coffee shops are there in the world, and what was it about Howard Schultz that allowed him to think of Starbucks as a global company—even when he had just four shops in Seattle?

How many thousands of shoe companies are there in the world, and what was it about Philip Knight that allowed him to think of Nike as a

---

[*] https://alibaba.brand.live/c/11-11

global company—even when he was selling shoes at track meets out of the trunk of his car?

This is a book about China, but one of the lessons is that a vision for China will work best when it is part of a global vision. Any successful China strategy will have two significant benefits for your company, for reasons unrelated to China:

First, going to China will help you expand and improve your business in your home market.

Second, success in China will be a critical part of your international strategy, enabling you as you enter other countries.

So, whether you are moving to best practices back home or you are playing offense on a global stage, here are some ways to harness your China learnings and success to make your company successful beyond China.

First, China is leading the e-commerce trends that will help you back home.

In every market in the world, among every customer segment in the world, e-commerce is taking market share away from traditional retail. Not only does e-commerce drive a brand's conversation in ways traditional retail cannot, it also drives consumer decision-making, defines a brand, and sets the pace for retail competition.

Digital marketing allows companies to selectively target and retain customers, social networks carve brand identity, and ease of payment on mobile phones translates to newfound purchasing power. Traditional retail lacks the transparency, price comparison capabilities, and customer reviews that online shoppers enjoy.

Developing your success in China allows you to experience e-commerce at its best, in a range of vital functions:

Marketing: Each month in China brings a new set of promotions and themes, and you need to align your marketing material and digital content with what's trending. Brands get stale quickly. Do you have products and bargains that are exclusive to your on-line channel? What would the cost and benefit be if you improved your promotional cadence and new product introduction from quarterly to monthly? How can you start experimenting with livestreaming in your home market?

Logistics: China expects same-day shipping in tier-one cities, with next day shipping for most of the rest of the country. This means any purchase in China can be an impulse purchase and e-commerce becomes the preferred channel. How can you put your home market on a one-day shipping footing, and what happens if your product is also viewed as an impulse purchase?

Customer service: In China, consumers expect thoughtful responses, high-quality engagement, and they want to be accommodated—all in real time. Can you benchmark your home market Customer Relationship Management response against your China team?

Developing your success in China helps your organization become a learning organization and improves your ability to adapt and experiment. You broaden and improve your model through variation, experimentation, and understanding the world around you.

This will help you compete at home, look for advantageous partnerships, and to stay ahead of your competitors.

Some of this adaptation has already started. Amazon Live's format is very much like Taobao Live. Facebook and Instagram are adapting so customers can make immediate transactions like Chinese customers can on TikTok, Kuaishou, and Little Red Book. And look to Walmart learning from its ownership stake in JD.com.

Second, China helps you develop skills and experience that can help in other international markets.

The emergence of a global middle-class means the emergence of global markets to an extent never before seen. Mid-tier companies can profitably run multi-country operations.

A brand's experience with China e-commerce can lead to other steps in new markets.

In some markets, there is a natural spillover in solutions. Alibaba owns Lazada, which is a group of six e-commerce platforms that serve Southeast

Asia markets. In the same vein, Amazon operates platforms in sixteen different markets. And traditional retailers such as Walmart and Aldi are multi-market. Your China success will let you have better conversations with Lazada, Amazon, and these other service providers about entering their markets.

Similarly, your experience in dealing with China logistics providers will be of assistance as you work with providers in new markets, and the same with your experience in monitoring currencies. You are not just building out a China team in your head office; you are building out an international team. The same process you used to evaluate cultural adaptation for China can be used for France, or Mexico, or any other market.

The same principle applies to trade finance. If a US firm sells $10 million annually of a cosmetic product into China, it can easily arrange financing from Chinese or American banks to support its inventory. But what about a firm that wants to enter the Indonesian market and its first-year sales are projected to be only $2,00,000? It probably wouldn't be cost-effective to try to arrange financing when major providers aren't interested. So why not set up financing that looks at a brand's performance globally, instead of requiring that credit lines be established in each market?

Until we meet again

I hope you have enjoyed the journey over these past 180 or so pages and I hope it inspires you to take your first steps, either by yourself or with partners. This is my final hope for you as we conclude this book, that you start to evaluate whether your brand might be a good fit for the China market. Please don't just leave this book on the shelf when you have finished. Perhaps you can pass it along to a colleague at work or schedule an office meeting to discuss China.

If you do start thinking seriously about China, let me know if I can help out. Maybe we'll run into each other at a trade show, or let me know if we can catch up on a swing through Europe or the United States. And you can meet our China team when you get to Shanghai.

Key Takeaways

➢ The world is not standing still.
➢ Please don't you stand still either.

Acknowledgements

A book on China e-commerce touches on topics ranging from China, to retail and consumer goods, to new market entry, and I am grateful in the course of writing this book that I was able to call on friends and associates for their advice and insight.

At my firm, Export Now, we had a number of conversations on this topic and I am thankful to. Katerina Cai, Tim Druzbik, Shannon Hughes, Kan Zhang, Mengdi Mi, and Celine Wu for their advice and encouragement.

I am thankful that a number of friends contributed thoughts: Shaun Rein, Joe Nora, Charlie Skuba, Brian Wong, Man-Chung Cheung, John Hackett, Edward Tse, Daniel Zipser, Danielle Bailey, Jim McGregor, and Ashley Dudarenok

And I am grateful to my wife Ann, who provided line editing and comments as did our children, Abby, Nat, and Liz. I am grateful to each of you for your keen eye and ideas.

I am grateful to Will Adamopoulos and Rob Olsen of Forbes Asia who first encouraged me to write about China e-commerce and also to David Feith of the Wall Street Journal where I shared some early thoughts.

I would like to thank Jiayi Zhong, my research assistant for helping with fact checking, footnotes, and additional thoughts on presentation and e-commerce.

Most of all I thank Dan Kadison, a 'book whisperer'. Dan can help shape a coherent book out of a variety of rough drafts, ideas, and fragments of ideas.

Special thanks to my agent Nick Wallwork who was relentlessly genial in refining the book concept and proposal and working with the publisher; to Nora Nazerene from Penguin Random House who believed in the idea of this book and shepherded it through to publication; to Amberdawn Manaois who meticulously edited the text and provided suggestions to improve its lucidity and readability; and to Usha Surampadi, who patiently provided the line edits.

Explanation of Terms

AI—Artificial Intelligence: The use of computer programs to model human behavior. AI in an on-line chat program can handle routing questions.

AR/VR—Augmented Reality and Virtual Reality: A cosmetics brand can start with real photos and use AR to illustrate how a person might look using different cosmetics.

B2B—Business to Business: When one business sells to another.

B2C—Business to Consumer: When a business sells to a consumer.

C2C—Consumer to Consumer: When individuals sell to each other.

CAPEX—Capital Expenditure: Up-front costs of plant and equipment that will allow the business to operate.

Daigous—Individual and small-scale merchants who buy goods overseas and resell in China. This is typically an informal or grey market activity which means that although the goods are authentic, the store is unofficial.

FOMO—Fear of Missing Out: A short-hand explanation of crowd behavior.

FTZ—Free Trade Zone: Part of a country's territory which is deemed to be outside of that country's customs system. A company can stage goods in an FTZ without paying duties.

GMV—Gross Merchandise Volume (sometimes referred to as Gross Merchandise Value): The most common sales measurement in e-commerce. GMV is calculated by multiplying the total volume of goods sold by the listed price of each good. In other words, it assumes there are no discounts or rebates. If you sell 10 items at $100 each, your GMV is $1000.

IP—Intellectual Property: The intangible assets of a company, such as brand value, or proprietary design.

J-Curve—A curve that first goes down before it goes up: This is a typical illustration of a company's profitability when it enters a new market. Initially it might lose money, but it eventually earns a profit.

Juhuasuan—Group sales or flash sales on the Alibaba Platform: This is a daily deal site which allows a brand to scale quickly but with reduced profitability.

KOL—Key Opinion Leader: These are the Internet celebrities who help sell products. In China, many have their own on-line channels or shows that allow them to demonstrate and discuss products.

MAU—Monthly Active Users: This is a measurement of people who have interacted with a web site within the past 30 days.

O2O—Online to Offline, also called Omnichannel: This is the strategy that allows brands to have an integrated online and offline presence so that the consumer can purchase through either channel with the same results.

P&L—Profit and Loss: A table of revenue and expenditures in a given time period.

PEO—Professional Employers Organization: An outsourcing firm that supplies services to small and medium-sized businesses.

TP—Tmall Partner: An approved e-commerce operator who can handle a range of activities to run your e-commerce stores in China.

CPSIA information can be obtained
at www.ICGtesting.com
Printed in the USA
LVHW011251041121
702389LV00001B/3

9 789814 954655